A Guide to Children's Poetry
for Teachers and Librarians

For Sue and Wyn

A Guide to Children's Poetry for Teachers and Librarians

Barrie Wade

SCOLAR PRESS

Published by
SCOLAR PRESS
Gower House
Croft Road
Aldershot
Hants GU11 3HR
England

Ashgate Publishing Company
Old Post Road
Brookfield
Vermont 05036-9704
USA

British Library Cataloguing in Publication Data

Wade, Barrie
 A guide to children's poetry for teachers and librarians
 1. Children's poetry, English – Bibliography
 I. Title
 016.821'008'0928

Library of Congress Cataloging-in-Publication Data

Wade, Barrie
 A guide to children's poetry for teachers and librarians / Barrie Wade
 Includes index.
 ISBN 1-85928-141-9 (cloth)
 1. Children's poetry—History and criticism.   I. Title
 PN1085.W33—1996
 809.1'0083—dc20   96-41852
                        CIP

ISBN 1-85928-141-9

Printed and bound in Great Britain by
Biddles Ltd, Guildford and King's Lynn

Contents

Notes on contributors   vi
Introduction   vii
Acknowledgements   viii
How to use this book   ix

Poetry collections   1
Anthologies   51
Poetry resource books   109
    Audio Tapes   128

Poetry contacts   131
    Arts councils   131
    Regional arts boards   132
    Poetry libraries and specialist organisations   133

The Poetry Society   135
Poetry Library   139
Northern Poetry Library   141
Scottish Poetry Library   143
Getting poetry published   144
Poetry competitions for children   145

Index of titles   147
Index of authors and editors   152
Thematic index   155

Notes on contributors

Editor

Barrie Wade has taught in primary, secondary and special schools, but for the last 20 years has worked in the School of Education, University of Birmingham. He is editor of *Educational Review* and adviser to the Poetry Society. He regularly works for the Poets for Schools scheme and has published seven collections of poetry, the latest being *Rainbow* (Oxford University Press, 1995) and *The Woodland* (Knighton Books, 1995).

Reviewers

Wendy Cooling taught English in Inner London secondary schools for many years and was seconded as an adviser on school libraries and reading. She went on to run the Children's Book Foundation, a charity concerned with the promotion of reading, and now works as a book consultant, reviewer and in-service trainer. She is an adviser to the Poetry Society and a member of the School Library Association's National Committee. Wendy has edited story collections for children and written many children's guides for the National Trust.

Trevor Dickinson taught English for 14 years in secondary schools in England and Canada before becoming English Adviser to Sheffield LEA in 1968. In 1971 he began a 20-year career as HMI, with a national library role in his last five years until retirement. He writes verse for children under a closely guarded pseudonym. He reviews regularly for *The School Librarian*, and has twice reviewed the Spring Picture books for *Books For Keeps*. In 1990 he was awarded the OBE for his work in promoting children's reading. In 1991 he was elected an Honorary Fellow of the Library Association.

Maggie Moore has been head of an Educational Assessment Unit after teaching mainstream primary classes. She is currently Senior Lecturer in Education at Newman College, Birmingham. She has written extensively on literacy and special educational needs and has also published twenty books for children.

Jack Ousbey has taught infant, junior and secondary pupils, students in a college of education, and adults for the WEA and Open University. He was the visiting adviser for The British School of Brussels, and continues to lead in-service events for teachers and librarians. He was an English adviser and Senior Inspector in Nottinghamshire, before taking a part-time post as a writer and consultant with an independent children's TV company. He has published six story books for young children and is currently editing a poetry anthology, *Exploding Poems*, to be published by Scholastic Children's Books in 1996.

Introduction

Children and adolescents take naturally to poetry. Poetry is a source of pleasure and satisfaction. Poems delight and entertain while giving insight into the way we and other people think. Very young children take naturally to rhythms and rhymes in both oral and written literature and several recent articles (including those published by the Poetry Society) show what older children can achieve in poetry – even those with special educational needs.

If there are any problems, these exist rather in the minds of adults who regard poetry as precious, difficult or to be worked through systematically for understanding. Children intuitively know that poems are not comprehension exercises, though sometimes they are treated as such. T.S. Eliot was right when he warned that poetry could communicate without necessarily being understood.

There is now a wealth of published poetry for children which communicates directly to both thoughts and feelings, but there is a need to widen the range of poetry with children's experience. Much now exists that many adults may be unaware of and therein lies the rationale of this book.

This volume sets out to survey poetry published for children and to provide a source of information for teachers, librarians and parents as well as for young people themselves. The information that is conveyed is of two kinds: first is factual information about titles, authors, prices and publishers; second is evaluative information provided by one of the experienced reviewers together with recommendations about the likely age range of readers for each book. Finally, there is further information about important contacts and resources for poetry, sections on specialist libraries, the Poetry Society, how to get poetry published and poetry competitions for children.

Inevitably there has been some selection by myself and the four reviewers and though most of what the publishers sent to us features in the following pages, there are bound to be errors and omissions. It is my hope that where these are noticed readers will write to Scolar Press and point them out so that they can, where relevant, be included in a future updated edition.

Acknowledgements

My admiration goes first to the four reviewers whose work is central to the pages that follow. I bombarded them with massive parcels of books and they never flinched. Well, maybe there was occasionally the temptation to run off to Prague or seek anonymity in football crowds, but this was never yielded to so far as I know. I was impressed by the speedy way in which they returned reviews as well as by their insight, perceptiveness and clarity.

I am grateful to all those publishers who sent me books for review. Without their help this volume could never have been written.

Finally I acknowledge the word-processing skills of Wyn Mills and Sue Bonser who produced sections of the book in its final form. Sue's organisational skills in manipulating and ordering both books and contents contributed to making the editing task a rewarding one for me.

How to use this book

The system of this book is essentially easy to follow. There are three main resource sections: single author collections, edited anthologies and resource books anthologies particularly designed for classroom use. Within each section, entries are arranged in alphabetical order by author or editor.

Each entry follows a similar pattern

Author or Editor
Title
Publication and biographical details
Review of book
Suggested age range of readers   initials of reviewer
Themes

The later sections of the book offer essential information on national and regional support for poetry, specialist collections, publication and poetry competitions. At the time of going to press details in these sections are correct, but will be brought up-to-date as necessary in future editions.

The title, author and thematic indexes provide a speedy source of information and cross referencing.

Poetry Collections

A

AGARD, John
The Calypso Alphabet
Picture Lions, 1989
28 pp, paperback, ISBN 0–00–663676–4
Notes on Caribbean words and phrases, colour line illustrations

Beginning with Anancy and ending with Zombie, John Agard takes 26 Caribbean words, or alliterative phrases, and through them introduces young readers to the colours and tastes, sights and sounds of the Islands. The short, rhythmic, rhyming text is well served by Jennifer Bent's strong pictures which gleam and glow as the pages are turned.

This is a book to stand alongside the best of alphabet books in your Infants' Library, and certainly one you will be using for reading aloud, and learning by heart.

Age range: 4–6 JO

AGARD, John
I Din Do Nuttin
Red Fox, 1993
48 pp, paperback, ISBN 0–09–918451–6
b/w illustrations

The rhythm, humour and real pictures of childhood in John Agard's poetry make this collection a must for all infant and primary schools. There are memories of the Caribbean and of England and a range of moods in these poems which really leap out and sparkle. Some, such as 'Happy Birthday, Dilroy!' have serious points to make. A collection not to be missed.

Age range: 5–11 WEC
Theme: Caribbean

AGARD, John
Say it Again Granny
Little Mammoth, 1990
42 pp (unnumbered), paperback, ISBN 0–7497–0747–X
Thematic, b/w line illustrations

This is a collection of twenty poems based on Caribbean proverbs. They are amusing and contain a lot of sense, for example, 'Don't call Alligator Long-Mouth till you cross river!' Some perhaps are more suitable for the urban way of life – 'Never stop to roll up yuh stocking when you running to catch train!' The proverbs are placed inside the poems which are reflections on what Granny says and the misunderstanding that can arise when they are taken literally. They need to be shared and talked about. They also need to be read out loud; they are a delight. Some are written in semi-dialect – good fun! – and lots of good sense. Illustrations by Susanna Gretz are sensitively and delicately drawn and illustrate the proverbs literally at times and, at others, the poems which contain them.

> Age range: 7–12 MM
> Themes: Proverbs/Sayings

ALBOROUGH, Jez

Where's My Teddy?
> Walker Books, 1992
> 24 pp, paperback, ISBN 0–7445–3058–X
> Colour line illustrations

Eddy loses his teddy one day and has to search in a frightening, dark wood to find him. There is a very big surprise in store for Eddy before his own toy is found again.

Jez Alborough's tale has a strong, rollicking rhythm, and rhymes that drop into place so easily that young children will be encouraged to join in at the first telling.

Amongst all the stories and poems about teddy-bears this one is sure to be a favourite with the very young, who will also enjoy the simple but effective illustrations.

> Age range: 4–6 JO
> Theme: Bears

ALLEN, Fergus

The Brown Parrots of Providencia
> Faber and Faber, 1993
> 66 pp, paperback, ISBN 0–571–17011–0
> Contents, no illustrations

This collection of poetry is very powerful. Many of the poems are dark, brooding, even bitter, but truthful. They provide comments on human experiences and reaction to those experiences, for example, 'Tanks in Moscow', which serve to highlight a lack of human connection and empathy that affects many of the population. There are lighter moments, for example 'The Fall' which substitutes the Garden of Eden for Guinness's Brewery!

It is a compact, complex collection which is more a collection for adults than children. 'A' level candidates would appreciate the poems; it is doubtful whether younger students would appreciate them.

> Age range: 16+ MM
> Theme: Human behaviour

ANDREW, Moira; DOHERTY, Berlie; COTTON, John; NICHOLLS, Judith; RICE, John; ROGERS, Paul

(a) ## Racing the Wind
> Nelson, 1993
> 24 pp, paperback, ISBN 0–17–400702–7
> Contents, colour illustrations

(b) ## Big bulgy fat black slugs
> Nelson, 1993
> 16 pp, paperback, ISBN 0–17–400708–6
> Contents, colour illustrations

(c) **First things**
Nelson, 1993
16 pp, paperback, ISBN 0–17–400707–8
Contents, colour illustrations

(d) **Jigglewords**
Nelson, 1993
16 pp, paperback, ISBN 0–17–400706–X
Contents, colour illustrations

(e) **Down at the Dinosaur Fair**
Nelson, 1993
24 pp, paperback, ISBN 0–17–400704–3
Contents, colour illustrations

(f) **Yuck!**
Nelson, 1993
24 pp, paperback, ISBN 0–17–400703–5
Contents, colour illustrations

These first poetry books are written by six established poets. There is interesting language in *Racing the Wind* by Moira Andrews and a great sense of movement, especially in the title poem. In *Big bulgy fat black slugs* Berlie Doherty uses lots of similes, onomatopœia and alliteration and words such as slimy, squashy, squelchy and slithery will really appeal when read with expression. John Cotton plays with words and gives moods to the days of the week in *First things*. The title poem in this book really gets children thinking and talking. Judith Nicholls has chosen to write poems about numbers and to introduce ideas about conservation in her gentle collection. John Rice's poetry is more wild and wacky and offers a real change of mood – children will love the dinosaur poems and illustrations. In *Yuck!*, Paul Rogers writes about all those horrible things that children love to read about – eating tadpoles and tummies full of sick!

The first, fifth and sixth titles are aimed at Year 1 and the rest at Year 2 but all these books would be useful in any infant classroom.

Age range: 4–7   WEC
General theme: Insects

ARMITAGE, Simon
Kid
Faber and Faber, 1992
88 pp, paperback, ISBN 0–571–16607–5
Contents, no illustrations

In 1989 Simon Armitage made a powerful impact on the poetry scene with his first publication, Zoom. His 1992 collection, Kid, opens with a mysterious poem about a visitor who disturbs the routines of family life. Like many of Armitage's poems it stays in the mind, releasing small insights as it is re-read or reconsidered. Armitage writes for the ear. Many of his poems – 'Catch', 'Looking for Weldon Kees', 'Not the Furniture Game', for instance – almost ask to be read aloud. Others are challenging enough to evoke a response from the reader, with their unexpected switches and sharp observations. And then there are the intriguing 'Robinson' poems, in which we follow the eponymous hero as he tries to cope with life in the mid-nineties. Kid is, in fact, a collection for the reader (of whatever age) who is interested in the social and political conditions of modern Britain.

The world according to Armitage is unfair, illogical, exhilarating, funny, frightening, mysterious and magical, and, with his effortlessly inventive style, he asks the reader to join him and take a look at what is happening to us all.

Age range: 16+   JO
Theme: Living in today's world

AUDEN, W.H. (edited by Edward MENDELSON)
Selected Poems
Faber and Faber, 1979
304 pp, paperback, ISBN 0–511–11396–6
Contents, Index, A note on the text, 12 Page Introduction, no illustrations

Auden suspected any poem of his which became a popular anthology piece and would not read that kind of poem to an audience. The first selected poems were chosen by the poet himself and favoured his later poetry: this collection, made by Edward Mendelson, contains one hundred poems, and offers an excellent survey of the poet's work.

Mendelson has written a short but excellent preface to the poems in which he outlines the poet's developing voice and considers his stature as a major 20th century poet. He defends his decision to print poems which Auden had later rejected or revised, and suggests that the best way to get to know his work is to read the earlier versions first for their greater immediate impact.

The selection includes work from all of Auden's books of verse and the arrangement is chronological. This is essential reading for anyone studying Auden's work, or for those students interested in seeing how his vision, both in terms of concept and style, fits into the history of modern poetics.

Age range: 16+   JO

AUDEN, W.H. (Wystan Hugh), (edited by Edward MENDELSON)
Collected Poems
Faber and Faber, 1976, revised/reset 1991, this issue 1994
925 pp, paperback, ISBN 0–571–14226–5, £14.99
Contents, Index of titles, first lines, Appendices detailing excluded titles, variant titles, no illustrations

In May 1995 Auden appeared as one of the firmly recommended 20th century poets in SCAA's Draft Proposals for English in the National Curriculum at both Key Stage 3 and Key Stage 4. For whatever reason he is absent from the January 1995 programmes of study. Perhaps someone read Anthony Thwaite's 'Poetry Today' which points to the disillusion some have grown to feel – especially with some of Auden's later work. That said, Auden will still have his devotees – and they will be well served by this massive, somewhat unwieldy collection of nigh on 340 poems. There is a brief introduction by the editor (Edward Mendelson) and a 2-page foreword by Auden himself (dating from 1944 and 1965). Both pieces throw useful light on Auden's poetic processes. For the Auden enthusiast this is clearly an impressive collection – but it is likely to be too daunting for those who are making their first approach to this poet.

Age range: 16+   TD

B

BECK, Ian
Little Miss Muffet
Oxford University Press, 1988
30 pp, paperback, ISBN 0–19–272215–8
Contents, colour line illustrations

Ian Beck gives this old favourite a new twist: instead of a spider sitting beside Miss Muffet a whole range of unexpected friends turn up to join her on the tuffet. The result is a fresh, amusing text with bright, simple illustrations which give a child's eye view of the action.

Children between the ages of 2–5 will enjoy taking part in these new adventures of Miss Muffet. This is a good book for sharing with an individual child, or a small group on the library carpet.

Age range: 4–6   JO

Theme: Insects

BLOOM, Valerie
Duppy Jamboree
Cambridge University Press, 1992
32 pp, paperback, ISBN 0–521–40909–8
Contents, Glossary, b/w illustrations

Illustrations by Michael Charlton give delicate, gentle humorous support to this collection of 14 poems by Jamaican-born poet, Valerie Bloom. Described on the cover as 'performance poems . . . written in modified Jamaican patois', there is no doubt that they would have extra strength in the mouths of readers secure in the speech patterns of the Caribbean. That said, with the aid of the simple glossary, able primary school readers will enjoy 'translating' these poems. They will appreciate the universal jokes – about ghosts, dentists, over-eating, etc. And they will learn something about language.

Age range: 8–10+   TD

Theme: Caribbean childhood experiences

BODY, Wendy and CULLIMORE, Stan
Illustrated by Rhian Nest James
Late Again, Mai Ling?
Longman, 1994
16 pp, paperback, ISBN 0–582–12356–9
Series: The Book Project, Thematic, colour illustrations

A delightful rhyming counting story describing Mai Ling in the morning – getting ready for school and in danger of being late. One of the 'Read-Aloud' books in Longman's The Book Project, this is so much more satisfying, in terms of both content and presentation, than so many reading scheme books.

Age range: 3–6   WEC

Themes: Counting, Getting up

BROWN, Richard
The Midnight Party
Cambridge University Press, 1993
56 pp, paperback, ISBN 0–521–44587–6
Series: Talk Poetry 1 & 2, Contents, Notes on performing the poems – 9 pages,
Introduction – 2 pages, b/w line illustrations

Richard Brown has written these 22 poems as performing pieces for younger children. Each title is followed by an indication as to how many voices should be used, and there are further notes, at the end of the volume, giving fairly precise instructions about the interpretation and performance of the pieces.

Included in the collection are chants, songs, oral stories, interviews, and incantations, with parts for two, three, four voices and more. The topics cover names and naming, the playground, winter, parties, nighttime, and the sea.

There are few collections of this kind available for use in schools and many teachers will welcome the opportunity to involve their classes in presentation work. The companion volume, *Whisked Away*, is written for older children.

Age range: 7–9   JO
Theme: Performance

BROWN, Richard
Whisked Away

Cambridge University Press, 1993
56 pp, paperback, ISBN 0–521–44588–4
Series: Talk Poetry 1 & 2, Contents, Introduction – 2 pages, Notes on how to perform the poems – 8 pages, b/w line illustrations

This is the second volume, written by Richard Brown, with the intention of involving older children in the group presentation of poetry. The format is exactly the same as *The Midnight Party* (see review above), with slightly longer and appropriately more difficult material.

You will find here poems about creation and the elements, seeking one's fortune, hazardous journeys, headlines, travellers and a Christmas Eve piece. The poet has written a set of notes offering advice about the introduction, interpretation and presentation of each poem.

Age range: 9–11   JO
Theme: Performance

BURGESS, Mark
Feeling Beastly – Funny Verse to Read Aloud

Mammoth, 1990
64 pp, paperback, ISBN 0–7497–0277–X
Contents, Thematic, b/w illustrations

Lots of beastly poems to read aloud and enjoy. Irreverent images of the animal world illustrated with great wit by the poet. This collection is a good one to help children to enjoy poetry and to give them a way in to the wide range of poems they will meet later. Also guaranteed to change the reader's views – who could dislike a wasp after learning:

> The humble wasp is much maligned,
> He really is extremely kind.
> Any chap in striped pyjamas
> Couldn't really mean to harm us.
> It's just he thinks he's still in bed,
> Mistakes his tail for his head –
> And doesn't mean to use his sting
> But only kiss us, silly thing.

Age range: 6–10   WEC
Theme: Animals

BURGESS, Mark
Can't Get to Sleep – Poems to Read at Bedtime

Mammoth, 1991
64 pp, paperback, ISBN 0–7497–0416–0
Contents, Thematic, b/w illustrations

A perfect book for bedtime reading, illustrated with charm and humour by the poet. There's so much for children to recognise in this collection – putting off going to bed for as long as possible, midnight feasts, listening to the clock, dreams and counting sheep.

There are also longer, story-poems, one about a highwayman called Thomas Turnip, a new view of Noah's Ark and the terrible noise Noah had to put up with and one of Santa Claus getting his delivery date wrong.

A good collection to read together and to laugh about.

Age range: 6–10   WEC

Theme: Bedtime

BURGESS, Mark
Feeling Peckish
Methuen Children's Books, 1991
63 pp, hardback, ISBN 0–416–16172–3
Contents, b/w line illustrations

This collection of rhymes and verse is both written and illustrated by Mark Burgess. The verses, all of them about food, are ideal for reading aloud. Some are just plain silly, ideal for the giggly audience, others contain words of warning (*Mandy*, for example, who 'hasn't any teef') while *Picknicking* (*sic*) and *The Midnight Fox* are evocative poems of sea places or suburban gardens.

A good mix. The illustrations complement the poems – they are simple yet effective.

Age range: 6–10   MM

Theme: Food

C

COPE, Wendy
Twiddling Your Thumbs
Faber and Faber, 1988
32 pp, paperback, ISBN 0–571–16537–0
Contents, colour illustrations.

Twiddling Your Thumbs is an illustrated collection of hand rhymes, great fun for either home or school. Children will quickly learn the rhymes and be involved in the reading and in the actions – they will in fact be having a really enjoyable time with a book. Wendy Cope's 'Note for Grown-Ups' at the beginning of the book suggests ways of using it and concludes that, 'The experience of sharing books with a loved adult is the best possible foundation for a lifetime as an enthusiastic reader. Phonics and flash cards and graded schemes may have their place but the really important thing is to learn to love books.' The pleasure of being involved in this book will start children off on the right path.

Age range: 2–8   WEC

Theme: Hand rhymes

COPE, Wendy
Serious Concerns
Faber and Faber, 1992
74 pp, paperback, ISBN 0–571–16705–5, £5.99
Contents, no illustrations

Over a third of the 59 poems in this slim volume range between two and ten lines. Mainly tightly rhymed and emphatically rhythmical, the poems have a bitter-sweet if not a plainly sour and negative tone – particularly where men are concerned. Throwaway end-lines tend to play for easy laughs in flip fashion. Sometimes there is a feeling of Cyril Fletcher

Odd-Odeness and an irritating negativity about life and, again, especially, about relationships with men. In contrast, there are a couple of gently touching poems – such as 'Legacy' and 'Names', which treat with death and aging.

In the main this is an undemanding collection, but it will appeal to those sometimes reluctant to tackle less frothy material.

Age range: 15+   TD

Themes: Love, Men, Relationships

COTTON, John
Oscar the dog and friends

Longman, 1994
24 pp, paperback, ISBN 0–582–12171–X
Series: The Book Project, colour line illustrations

This is a book about dogs, many of the poems are about Oscar, who tells his own stories with the exception of the last. John Cotton gives his dogs different identities and personalities. Perhaps the most colourful is 'Sexton the Bloodhound' whose criminal hunting exploits are told with strong rhythm and rhyme, slightly reminiscent of Eliot's *Cats*.

Adrienne Geoghegan's illustrations are colourful and complement the given personalities.

Age range: 6–9   MM

Theme: Dogs

COWLING, Sue
What is a Kumquat?

Faber and Faber, 1991
50 pp, paperback, ISBN 0–571–16065–4
Contents, b/w line illustrations

Sue Cowling presents a variety of poetry for children. It's a good mixture of fantasy and stupidity which children will love, plus the poems that deal with issues that confront readers and make them think, reflect and talk about. 'Elephant Child' for example which focuses on ivory poaching, 'Requiem for a Robin' or 'Jeopardy' (losing a job). These poems are perhaps made stronger as they are islands in a sea of fun. More fun comes in the exploration and play with words. 'What *is* a Kumquat?', for example, or 'Waiting' which contains words not usually found in the English language. Illustrations by Gunver Edwards are quick, brief and realistic.

Age range: 8–14   MM

Themes: Animals, Childhood, Word Play

CROSSLEY-HOLLAND, Kevin
Beowulf

Oxford University Press, 1982
46 pp, paperback, ISBN 0–19–272184–4
Guide to Pronunciation, b/w line illustrations

Perfectly illustrated by Charles Keeping in monochrome pictures of great power, this is an excellent re-telling of the eighth-century poem. Kevin Crossley-Holland writes prose which is invested with the dramatic rhythms and dynamics of poetry, and which retains a strong sense of period.

> The great sea-bird rode on the breakers. And as soon as the Geats hoisted a sail,
> a bleached sea-garment, the boat foamed at the prow and surged over the waves.

The story of Beowulf ought to feature on the curriculum of all top juniors and, along with Serrailliers version and Rosemary Sutcliff's 'Dragon Slayer', this particular account is very strongly recommended. Serialised over a number of days this story would be an excellent one for re-telling and re-writing, with groups planning, drafting, illustrating and publishing their own bound manuscripts – perhaps in simulated leather, with marbled end-papers and bejewelled covers. Lovely! The stuff of real education.

Age range: 10–13   JO

Theme: Beowulf

CUNLIFFE, John
Dare You Go?

André Deutsch, 1992

64 pp, hardback, ISBN 0–590–54020–3, £7.99

b/w line illustrations

There is an even mix here of both sturdily rhymed and full verse, the latter especially ringing Michael Rosen bells. Helped by some attractive, amusing and sometimes reflective black and white illustrations by Michael Beach, this slim collection will do more good than harm – although some teachers and parents will be irritated by the occasional references to pee, farts and bums! In the main, the variety of mood, tone and verse technique results in a useful if not essential collection by the author of 'Postman Pat'.

Age range: 10–12   TD

Themes: Ghosts, Poetry, School

CURRY, Jennifer and FARROW, Rob (compiler)
I Remember, I Remember

Red Fox, 1993

187 pp, paperback, ISBN 0–09–931831–8, £3.50

Contents, Index of poets, of titles, of first lines, b/w illustrations

Sold in aid of the Malcolm Sargent Cancer Fund for Sick Children, this is a collection of some 105 'famous people's favourite childhood poems'. It has a certain curiosity value – the discovery for instance, that Dame Barbara Cartland and Paul Gascoigne both have chosen poems written by themselves. Virginia Bottomley's Belloc choice has a brief medical flavour. Baroness Thatcher goes for Kipling's 'Glory of the Garden' – with Lord Archer a Kipling fan too. Glenys Kinnock chooses Wilfred Owen; John Major 'The Jackdaw of Rheims.' In fact, Kipling makes nine appearances, Hopkins six, Belloc four – and Anon eight. In addition to those mentioned above, there are such luminaries as David Gower, Bobby Charlton, Peter Ustinov, Mary Whitehouse, Norman Lamont, Tony Benn and Linford Christie.

Much of what is here is very familiar and more attractively presented elsewhere; but may have, as noted earlier, a curiosity value for some young readers.

Age range: 11–16   TD

Themes: Animals, Death, Life, Magic, Mystery, People, Places, Travel, Weather

D

DOHERTY, Berlie

Walking on Air
Lions, 1993
90 pp, paperback, ISBN 0–00–674442–7
Contents, b/w line illustrations

Berlie Doherty's first collection is an excellent assortment of childhood dreams, desires and fantasies. It evokes childhood memories and invites the reader into a shared understanding. The use of language is simple yet dramatic; not all of the poems are comfortable as they deal with the cruelty of nature, memories and children themselves.

The collection has a wide variety of topics well written and accessible, a delight to share and read aloud.

Illustrations by Janna Doherty are delicate and unobtrusive. Highly recommended.
Age range: 8–14   MM
Themes: Children, Feelings, Memories

DUNMORE, Helen

Secrets: A collection of poems from hidden worlds
The Bodley Head, 1994
64 pp, paperback, ISBN 0–370–31882–X
Contents, no illustrations

The secrets of the title refer to the hidden worlds beneath the surface of everyday lives. Many of the poems tell stories – for example, what was happening in the mind of one person before a bomb exploded on an underground railway platform; another traces the plight of the homeless. The collection offers a mixture of realism and fantasy and none of the poems give up their secrets easily; the discovery depends on what the reader brings to the poem. Helen Dunmore explains her purposes in a letter to the reader. A fascinating and powerful collection.
Age range: 12–16   MM
Theme: Secrets

E

EDWARDS, Richard
Illustrated by Sarah Fox-Davies

Moon Frog
Walker Books, 1992
45 pp, hardback, ISBN 0–7445–2157–2
Index, colour illustrations

This is an unusual collection of animal poems. The mood of the poems and the pictures is very varied and the animals are not always the ones poets choose to write about. The first poem, 'This Wasp', really takes young readers into the book and the images offered of porcupines, kangaroos, herons, hippos, etc. are unexpected. The rhythm in 'Midnight', the fun in 'Ozzie Octopus' and the magic of 'Moon Frog' delight children and make them want to return to this book again and again.
Age range: 4–8   WEC
Theme: Animals

EDWARDS, Richard

The Word Party

Lutterworth Press, 1986
64 pp, hardback, ISBN 0–7188–2649–3
Contents, b/w illustrations

The opening poem in this collection reads:

> When I was three I had a friend
> Who asked me why bananas bend,
> I told him why, but now I'm four
> I'm not so sure . . .

and really entices young readers into the book which goes on to deliver the fun and enjoyment it promises. The excitement of the child in 'Snow' is almost tangible and it's easy to see the 'Littlemouse' as he goes,

> Scrabbling and tripping,
> Sliding and slipping,

across the field. Richard Edwards has such a sure touch that his poems become pictures and John Lawrence's enchanting illustrations give them even more life.

A good collection for top primary/lower secondary readers, for reading aloud and sharing – it will turn many on to poetry.

Age range: 8–12   WEC

EDWARDS, Richard

Whispers from a Wardrobe

Lutterworth Press, 1987
64 pp, hardback, ISBN 0–7188–2683–3
Contents, b/w illustrations

A fun collection of poems for children and parents to read together. There are lots of jokes that will really appeal as well as some quite sensitive ideas such as giving feelings to the snowdrop and the tree.

> Who?
> I'm sure it wasn't me who spoke
> When I was shinning up the oak,
> So who, as I climbed up that tree
> Said, 'Get those nasty feet off me!'

There are riddles and rhymes, strange creatures and fantastic journeys intermingled with poems such as 'Sunlight or Surprise' which invites the reader to forget the myths about tramps and think of them as real people. Young readers will get the message of 'Why', an imaginative reminder of their own, probably endless questions.

Richard Edwards uses rhyme to good effect and offers a collection full of laughter, warmth and ideas to think about.

Age range: 8–12   WEC

ELIOT, T.S.

Old Possum's Book of Practical Cats

Faber and Faber, first published 1939, new edn 1953, retitled *The Illustrated Old Possum*, 1974
64 pp, paperback, ISBN 0–571–13644–3
b/w and colour line illustrations

This longstanding favourite is good to re-read and renew acquaintance. The strong rhythm, rhyme and narrative quality makes each poem ideal for reading aloud to children and drawing them into the world of strange and mysterious cats. The book is also ideal to curl up with for private reading.

The illustrations by Nicolas Bentley are still fresh and up to date and add an air of sophistication and elegance which children will appreciate.

Age range: 6–16   MM

Theme: Cats

ELIOT, T.S.

Collected Poems: 1909–1962

Faber and Faber, 1936
238 pp, paperback, ISBN 0–571–10548–3
Contents, Index, no illustrations

This collection, like the majority of Faber's poetry publications, contains a contents list, the poems themselves and an index. Anyone wishing to teach the texts is left to find commentaries, and devise assignments and study programmes, in a way appropriate to the individual and his/her students.

This edition, first published in 1936, includes: Prufrock; Poems 1920; The Waste Land; The Hollow Men; Ash Wednesday; Ariel Poems; Unfinished Poems, and a group of minor poems; plus choruses from 'The Rock'. The Four Quartets, and some Occasional Verses. There is also a CIP record available from The British Library.

Age range: 16+   JO

ESBENSEN, Barbara Juster

Words with Wrinkled Knees

Oxford University Press, 1990
44 pp, hardback, ISBN 0–19–276100–5
Contents, Thematic, b/w illustrations

A most unusual and special book of animal poetry made even better by John Stadler's bold and creative pictures. The page layout is attractive and very clear with one beautifully illustrated poem to the double page. Animal names are given their own personalities and developed into poems in a quite extraordinary way. For example: ELEPHANT is 'a word with wrinkled knees and toes like boxing gloves', HIPPOPOTAMUS 'It sinks if you look at it, sinks into mud at the bottom of warm rivers' and of course there's PENGUIN 'Best-dressed word in the world atlas!' The look of the poems (spaces in the middle of lines and the use of capital letters) adds to the effect and gives a sense of movement. The poems need to be read several times if all the teasing and joking are to be enjoyed and if the pictures that really catch the mood of the poems are to be appreciated.

Age range: 7–12   WEC

Theme: Animals

EWART, Gavin
Like it or Not
Red Fox, 1993
64 pp, paperback, ISBN 0–09–910521–7
Contents, Thematic, b/w illustrations

Gavin Ewart writes with wit and humour about likes and dislikes and these poems will surely appeal to the young. They will enjoy the games he plays with words – and rhymes such as 'few pence' and 'nuisance' in 'What People Think About Children'. The rhyme, although different in pattern, is very strong in all these poems; so it's good to use this book alongside other collections to reinforce the fact that poetry doesn't have to rhyme.

Age range: 7–11   WEC

Theme: Likes and dislikes

F

FORBES, Duncan
Poems That Point the Finger
Bodley Head, 1994
80 pp, paperback, ISBN 0–370–31816–1
Contents, no illustrations

Duncan Forbes writes about shared personal concerns such as love, death, anger and fear as well as about more public, more political issues. There is some humour in the poems but the central mood is uncompromising and confrontational. His language is sensitive and yet very strong whether he's inviting the reader to think about the death of a bee or about Maggie Thatcher and John Major. This is a book to browse through; a book in which to find connections. The experience of sibling competition so many will recognise, is movingly described in 'Sister' and the observation in 'The Way Things Are' also strikes a chord. There are poems that make one feel slightly uncomfortable – it's outrageous to think that the experience with the beggar, so powerfully described in 'The Touch', is a very common one – and just a few, such as 'Postcard', to smile at. The poems are well-crafted and very varied in this provocative collection for older readers.

Age range: 13+   WEC

Themes: Anger, Fear, Death, Love

FOSTER, John
Four o'clock Friday
Oxford University Press, 1991, this printing 1994
64 pp, paperback, ISBN 0–19–276093–9, £2.99; hardback, ISBN 0–19–276090–4
Contents, b/w illustrations

Just short of 60 poems here, illustrated in neat black and white by Debbie Cook, see John Foster in the rôle of poet rather than anthologiser. He offers verse tightly rhymed and steadily rhythmed; he offers verse free of these reins. There is the odd poetic joke alongside the serious reflection on important issues. There is a sense of a writer enjoying the artful craft of writing. Above all, without patronising young readers, John Foster is pretty successful in his attempt to draw them into the poetry fold.

Age range: 8–12+   TD

Themes: Childhood, Family, Family breakdown, Environmental issues, Nonsense, School, Sport

G

GERAS, Adèle
Josephine and Pobble
Longman, 1994
32 pp, paperback, ISBN 0–582–12161–2
Series: The Book Project, Thematic, colour line illustrations

The book contains two poems about cats; one is Josephine, a slightly up-market café cat and the other is Pobble, the Majestic Hotel cat. Josephine is elderly and tells of the activities of one snowy day in a café and of the people she meets. Her interest is no longer of chasing but of cream and eating. Pobble, the hotel cat, is much more active. Teresa O'Brien's illustration helps to give more depth and humour to some of the lines, for example;

I admire the shine on a pair of shoes

shows the cat with a shoe in a cat-wrestler's grip! Cats' movements and habits are well observed. The content sits uneasily between narrative and reflection; however, there are some lines that capture description:

the slow snow moths are falling again

and almost serve to make some illustrations superfluous.

Age range: 6–9   MM
Theme: Cats

GERAS, Adèle
Mimi and Apricot Max
Longman, 1994
32 pp, paperback, ISBN 0–582–12214–7
Series: The Book Project, Thematic, colour line illustrations

The book has two poems; one about a cat called Mimi and the other about a cat called Apricot Max – both are told from the cat's perspective.

They call me Mimi.

Mimi is bored during one rainy day, Apricot Max is the school cat who comforts little boys and wanders into lessons.

The poems contain some evocative and descriptive sections which, unfortunately, do not always match the content.

The illustrations by Teresa O'Brien are well observed and delicately drawn in beautiful detail.

Age range: 6–9   MM
Theme: Cats

GERRARD, Roy
Croco'Nile
Gollancz, 1994
32 pp, hardback, ISBN 0–575–05600–2
Colour line illustrations

Croco'Nile is set in Ancient Egypt, long ago, and tells the story of Hamut and his sister Nekatu, who have a series of amazing adventures, and are saved from an untimely end by a crocodile they once befriended.

The fast-moving rhyming tale is most beautifully illustrated by the author, with details which engage and inform as well as amuse the reader. Gerrard's stories (see also *Rosie and the Rustlers*) are recommended for use with junior age children.

Age range: 7–11   JO

Themes: Animals, Crocodiles

GERRARD, Roy

Jocasta Carr, Movie Star

Gollancz, 1992

30 pp, hardback, ISBN 0–575–05118–3, £7.99

Colour illustrations

This book is worth having for Roy Gerrard's marvellous full-colour illustrations alone. The fact that they exist to support his entertainingly extravagant verse tale of Jocasta Carr and her dog-napped co-star, Belle, makes them all the more worth while. In addition, Jocasta's brave efforts to rescue Belle from Maxwell Pym, the villainous producer, take young readers through interesting geographical territory – including New York, London, Africa, India. The verse through which Roy Gerrard tells this tale is bright, bouncy with a lovely kind of pomposity about it that adds well to the fun. What is more there is nothing here that patronises young readers.

Age range: 9–12+   TD

Theme: Adventure

GERRARD, Roy

Mik's Mammoth

Gollancz, 1993

32 pp (unnumbered), paperback, ISBN 0–575–05442–5

Thematic, Illustrations

Mik's Mammoth, written and illustrated by Roy Gerrard, is a delightful narrative poem in a picture book format. It tells the story of Mik, the less than fierce caveman, who, deserted by his tribe, uses his intelligence to adapt to his environment and eventually saves the tribe from disaster. He is helped in this and other ventures by Rumm the baby mammoth who Mik had found and rescued from the snow.

The poem charts the growing friendship and harmonious relationship between the two. The finely drawn and detailed illustrations capture this relationship and also chart the growth of Rumm from baby to giant. They also give a potted history of the civilising process of stone-age man, capturing the vast emptiness of the world, in contrast with the cosiness of the cave (complete with cave paintings!).

The poem is exciting to read aloud as it has a strong rhythm and definite rhyming pattern – both poem and illustrations need to be shared.

A good find.

Age range: 6–12   MM

Themes: Cave men, Mammoths, Stone-age

GERRARD, Roy

Rosie and the Rustlers

Gollancz, 1992

32 pp, paperback, ISBN 0–575–05209–0

Colour line illustrations

Roy Gerrard has cornered the market in dramatic monologues for younger children, and what great fun they are. His stories take account of the young reader's need for action and pace, and are lovingly, amusingly illustrated by the author himself.

Rosie and the Rustlers tells the tale of Rosie Jones, a ranch boss, and her hired hands, on the trail of a dastardly band of rustlers. They are helped by:

> Hawkeye John, the Indian Chief, said he'd help them track the thief,
> And his braves would guard the ranch while they were gone;
> So they set off there and then on the trail of Greasy Ben,
> And their hazardous adventure was begun.

These are ideal books for reading aloud, preferably to small groups so that the pictures can be enjoyed. Teachers with dramatic tendencies will love them, but they may operate most successfully when two or three children entertain each other, as they chuckle at the pictures and recite the stirring adventure.

Age range: 7–10   JO
Theme: Cowboys

GERRARD, Roy
The Favershams
Gollancz, 1993
32 pp, paperback, ISBN 0–575–05660–6
Colour illustrations

This verse narrative, written and brilliantly illustrated by Roy Gerrard, really is a picture book for all ages. The tongue-in-cheek biography of Charles Augustus Faversham satirises as it imitates the seriousness of Victorian biography. The life of the patriotic, caring family-man is revealed with dead-pan humour and astonishing pictures that deserve to be looked at again and again.

A very original and special book for every school library and home.

Age range: All ages   WEC
Theme: Victorian families

GIBSON, Miles
Say Hello to the Buffalo
Methuen, 1994
63 pp, hardback, ISBN 0–434–97557–5, £6.99
Contents, b/w illustrations

Forty poems on animals with well-observed black and white illustrations by Chris Reddell. The emphasis is mainly upon the comic; the mode is tightly rhymed and rhythmed verse, highly skilled. There's likely to be an enthusiastic reception for this new collection's refreshing approach to animals familiar and strange. Well-used, it could be a happy stimulus to writing by children.

Age range: 10–13+   TD
Themes: Animals, Insects

GREENLAW, Lavinia
Night Photograph
Faber and Faber, 1993
54 pp, paperback, ISBN 0–571–16894–9, £5.99
Contents, no illustrations

There is more of virtue than of vice about this slim first collection. Despite free-versish formats, there is a careful crafting about the short poems. Nonetheless, the pervasive conversational tone does not reduce the impenetrable opaqueness of so much of the content. My suspicion is that, although there are some very effective poems here and a freshness of observation and image, the collection as a whole will do little to enhance young people's appetite for poetry.

Age range: 16+   TD

Themes: Science, Environmental issues, Human behaviour

GROSS, Philip
The All-Nite Café

Faber and Faber, 1993
43 pp, paperback, ISBN 0–571–16753–5
Contents, no illustrations

The All-Nite Café was the winner of the Signal Poetry Award (1994) and it is easy to understand why. The collection encompasses inventive and imaginative treatment of many themes. The fear that is hidden in people and places is explored in many poems, – 'Multi-storey', 'Nightschool', for example, while in others, such as the 'All-Nite Café', a very alarming clientele is rendered harmless by its humorous treatment. The collection has numerous ghosts and hauntings.

Sea Changes is a 9-poem theme which explores environmental issues in a novel and thought-provoking way while 'Song of the Punk Mermaids' reminds the reader of the plight of the sea.

Amusing, frightening, complex – an excellent collection for sharing and reflection.

Age range: 11+   MM

Themes: Environment, Night, The Sea

H

HARRISON, Michael
Junk Mail

Oxford University Press, 1993
64 pp, paperback, ISBN 0–19–276113–7
Contents, b/w illustrations

An intriguing collection of poems full of word play, humour and provocative ideas. The book looks as if it's intended for quite young children and yet lots of the poems are rather sophisticated in terms of both ideas and humour and require the reader's serious thought and commitment. The opening poems are fun, off-beat letters to nursery rhyme and fairy tale characters but towards the end the poet addresses very serious issues in poems such as 'Thomas', 'Sunday Fathers', 'The Somme Battlefield' and 'Junk Mail'. Michael Harrison's poetry is clever, thought-provoking and at times lyrical and has a lot to offer to readers up to the lower years of secondary school. Sadly, however, some of them may be put off by the young look of the book.

Age range: 8–12   WEC

HAYES, Sarah
Illustrated by Helen Craig

This is the Bear

Walker Books, 1986
24 pp, paperback, ISBN 0–7445–0969–6
Series: This is the Bear books, colour line illustrations

There must be dozens of stories which use the structure and rhythms of 'The House that Jack Built' as a model, but few which do it as well as Sarah Hayes and her illustrator Helen Craig. Like all good translations this one achieves an originality of its own. The three central characters are lively, appealing and amusing; the plot and dénouement satisfying and unexpected.

This attractive book is sure to be popular with 2–5-year-olds and is very strongly recommended for reading aloud and sharing with nursery and play groups.

Age range: 2–5   JO
Theme: Bears

HAYES, Sarah
Illustrated by Helen Craig

This is the Bear and the Picnic Lunch

Walker Books, 1989
22 pp (unnumbered), paperback, ISBN 0–7445–1304–9
Colour line illustrations

A lovely story, told through a cumulative rhyme, about a boy, his dog, his bear and his missing picnic lunch. Good for reading aloud and sharing. The illustrations by Helen Craig complement and add extra dimension to the story – often with dialogue, 'Greedy Bear', 'Bad dog'.

The rhyme is simple and ideal for early readers – one that will be asked for again and again.

Age range: 3+   MM
Theme: Picnics

HAYES, Sarah
Illustrated by Helen Craig

This is the Bear and the Scary Night

Walker Books, 1991
32 pp, paperback, ISBN 0–7445–3147–0
Colour illustrations

The story of a boy, a dog and a bear – the bear is left overnight in the park, dropped into a pond by an owl, but is eventually rescued and reunited with his friends. The rhythmic text again follows the style of 'The House that Jack Built'. The vocabulary is simple, the story is enchanting and Helen Craig's beautiful illustrations make this a special book. Very young children will love to have it read to them over and over again; they will pick up the rhythm and soon join in using the pictures as prompts if necessary. The expressions on the bear's face, particularly when he's rescued from the pond, will encourage young children to really look at the pictures.

This book, with its large, bold print is ideal for very young children who will respond to the clear rhyme and rhythm of the text.

Age range: 1–6   WEC/MM
Theme: Bears

HENRI, Adrian
Dinner with the Spratts and other poems
Methuen, 1993
73 pp, hardback, ISBN 0–416–18855–9
Contents, b/w line illustrations

A very interesting collection of poems by Adrian Henri which is ably supported by the illustrations of Tony Ross. Many of the poems are humorous with a direct appeal to children; 'The Further Adventures of Sammy the Flying Piglet', for example, or 'I Saw' (a dinosaur). Yet Adrian Henri also addresses serious issues that concern the young. There is a focus on the environment, 'Dusty Bluebells', 'Song of the Earth', 'Rosie the Rhino', another for Oxfam – 'The Magic Mountain'. The concerns, however, are placed in poetry that is accessible to the reader.

Individual concerns are set within a sympathetic yet matter-of-fact context, for example the problem of being shortsighted, ('Out of Focus'), or frightened, ('Sticks and Stones') and lonely ('Children's Ward').

No collection for children would be complete without ghosts and we have them here – guaranteed to raise the hairs on the neck.

Age range: 7–12   MM
Themes: Environmental issues, Fear, Ghosts

HENRI, Adrian
The Phantom Lollipop Lady
Mammoth, 1986
96 pp, paperback, ISBN 0–7497–0227–3
b/w illustrations

Many of these poems show Adrian Henri at his most inventive and amusing. He makes a poem from cutting up bits of an issue of *Beano*; he writes about alien visitors, flying piglets, and nightmares in a cemetery; he dedicates poems to schools he has visited and he exercises his imagination on a swordfish without a nose and a versifying shellfish.

This is a small, pocketable paperback. Teachers of top juniors should carry it with them to read when things get too serious, or Maths problems too difficult, or Ofsted Inspectors too curious. As Henri puts it.

> Lives of shellfish all remind us
> We should make our life sublime;
> And, departing, leave behind us
> Claw-prints on the sands of time.

Age range: 9–13   JO
Themes: Animals, Fairy Tales, School

HENRI, Adrian
Illustrated by Tony Ross
Rhinestone Rhino
Methuen, 1989
72 pp, hardback, ISBN 0–416–06332–2
Contents, b/w illustrations

This slim volume is a delight as it offers so much to enjoy and to think about – the poems reveal Adrian Henri in many moods, writing in many styles. He writes of love, food, animals, other people and of war. He is never heavy handed and yet the poems, such as 'Shazia', which touches on the subject of racism and the five scenes in 'Wartime Child', offer much to discuss. Adrian Henri's poetry has the ability to touch the reader, to cause tears as well as laughter. The poems are good to read aloud, sometimes in parts as in 'Gordon Bennett' and 'The Heart Poem'.

The Tony Ross illustrations perfectly reflect the mood of the poems.

Age range: 8–12   WEC

Themes: Animals, Food, Love, People, War

HILL, Susan
Illustrated by Angela Barrett
Can it be True?
Walker Books, 1988 hbk, 1990 pbk, this reprint 1993
36 pp, paperback, ISBN 0–7445–1721–4, £3.99
Colour illustrations

The praises heaped upon this Smarties Book Prize winner on its first appearance continue to be fully justified. There is a sense, throughout this evocation of Christmas Eve, of a skilled writer savouring language on both tongue and ear. Engaging rhythmic control combines with gentle use of rhyme and half-rhymes to ensure a neatly compelling narrative flow. The whole book is elegantly produced, its print helpfully bold, its illustrations (by Angela Barrett) beautifully, richly complementary. This is a real treasure house of words and pictures.

Age range: 7–11+   TD

Theme: Christmas

HOBAN, Russell
Illustrated by Lillian Hoban
The Pedalling Man
Heinemann, 1969, this edition 1991
64 pp, hardback, ISBN 0–434–94214–6, £7.95
Contents, illustrations

Initially published in 1969, this edition, illustrated by Lillian Hoban, appeared in 1991 with 13 additional poems – making 40 in all. First time around, *The Guardian* critic described Russell Hoban as: 'A genuine poet of individual flavour'. There can be no need to revise that opinion. The vision that produces his fine fiction is apparent here too – as is his elegant manipulation of language and form, his inventive imagery that forces the reader to re-examine the world. But, despite a surface ease, demands are made of readers: this is, as a collection, not an easy option volume.

Age range: 12+   TD

Themes: Animals, Childhood, People, Places

HOUSTON, Libby
All Change
Oxford University Press, 1993
100 pp, hardback, ISBN 0–19–276064–5, £8.95
Contents, List of source books, b/w illustrations

This is a collection of 35 poems centring mainly on different kinds of transformation, and largely commissioned for BBC Schools Radio Broadcasts over a period of some 20 years. It may be that they broadcast better than they read on the page, but, despite the wide variety of forms represented – song, narrative, long, short, comic and serious – it is difficult to recommend this book to primary schools (which is where the publisher's flyer suggests it belongs). Few primary-aged children are likely to be drawn to poetry by this book – although some of the poems do explore interesting territory such as Hindu and Greek mythology and British Folk Tales. The main impression, however, is, too frequently, of an unsatisfactory and dissatisfying prosiness.

Age range: 9–11   TD
Themes: Greek/Indian Legend, Nature, Nonsense

HUGHES, Shirley
The Nursery Collection
Walker Books, 1994
62 pp, hardback, ISBN 0–7445–3210–8
Contents, no illustrations

Shirley Hughes is a great favourite with many very young children and this book will be loved as it brings together five books – *Bathwater's Hot*, *When We Went to the Park*, *Colours*, *All Shapes and Sizes* and *Noisy* – into one delicious volume. The story/rhymes introduce concepts of shape, size, opposites, number and colour in Shirley Hughes's warm and reassuring style. A lively toddler, so well observed, and her baby brother are the central characters in this big and beautiful picture book which is always child-centred. The lively young characters really add to the rhymes that children will want to listen to, and join in with, as often as the adult reader can stand!

Age range: 1–6   WEC
Theme: Early concepts

HUGHES, Shirley
Out and About
Walker Books, 1990
48 pp, paperback, ISBN 0–7445–1422–3
Colour illustrations

Shirley Hughes's books are always child-centred; her poems and illustrations draw children into a warm, reassuring world. The poems reflect her knowledge of children who really do love wind, puddles and mud, water and sand, food, fire and bedtime. The poems are for reading aloud and for sharing, and the pictures, especially the wordless double-page spreads, offer a lot to talk about. This is a beautiful picture poem book that celebrates so many simple things so dear to very young children. Perfect for bedtime reading and for the nursery/reception class.

Age range: 3–7   WEC
Themes: Bedtime, Fire, Food, Puddles and mud, Water and sand, Wind

HUGHES, Ted
Moon-Whales
Faber and Faber
92 pp, paperback, ISBN 0–571–16320–3
Contents, Thematic, b/w line illustrations

This paperback edition, first published in 1991, takes the reader straight into the strange, menacing moon-world of Ted Hughes's imagination, where moon-whales

Plough through the moon-stuff
Just under the surface,
Lifting the moon's skin
Like a muscle,

where burrow-wolves live in moon-holes, where moon-beggars screech and sob and suffer, and the Silent Eye floats up and gazes at passers-by like a drooping mourner.

Hughes has a deft, compelling touch as he wanders through the lunar landscape, illuminating the weird objects he meets with striking images:

> Tulips on the moon are a kind of military band;
> A bed of crimson ones will march up to your window and take its stand.
> Then out of their flashing brass and silver they rip some Prussian fanfare.

This kind of collection would repay study by a Year 7 or 8 class leading, perhaps, to a group presentation of the poems. A rich, challenging collection, the kind of thing Hughes does so brilliantly when writing for children.

Age range: 9–13   JO
Theme: Moon

HUGHES, Ted
Meet My Folks!
Faber and Faber, 1987
61 pp, paperback, ISBN 0–571–13644–3
Contents, Thematic, b/w line illustrations

Ted Hughes invites the reader to meet his most peculiar family; there's something odd about all of them. Sister Jane, for example, is a crow. One grandma knits outfits for wasps (to give them a colour change), goldfish (to keep them warm in winter) and for camels. The illustrations by George Adamson detail all these peculiarities and make references to other family members mentioned in the poem. One or two are more disturbing than others, for example, 'My Aunt Flo', who is lovely by day but raids grave-yards by night and will travel 300 miles for a new-buried baby. Although first published in 1961 they have some of the Dahl-like qualities that children enjoy so much.

Age range: 8–14   MM
Theme: Family

HUGHES, Ted
Season Songs
Faber and Faber, 1976, revised 1985
80 pp, paperback, ISBN 0–571–13703–2, £3.99
Contents, no illustrations

This slim volume has lost none of its appeal since its 1976 appearance. The four seasons are separately represented by poems which have the hallmarks of Ted Hughes's sharpest observational powers and linguistic energy. There is humour here; there is food for thought; there is pathos. Accessibility of language in no way diminishes its quality in a collection which rewards both the ear and the imaginative eye.

Age range: 11+   TD
Themes: Nature, Seasons

HUGHES, Ted
Selected Poems 1957–1981
Faber and Faber
238 pp, paperback, ISBN 0–571–119–166
Contents, no illustrations

This selection was made by the poet himself and draws on all the major collections published between 1957 and 1981. It provides a comprehensive view of Hughes's achievements and developing skills, and is essential reading for students looking at his poetry.

The poet's chosen themes are all here – animals, the weather, birth and death, the violent energies of the non-human world – and from *Season Songs*, poems which celebrate the changing year on the farm. The latter (along with *The Iron Man* and *Meet My Folks!*) makes an excellent introduction to Hughes's work for younger children.

All the epithets written about Ted Hughes are applicable some of the time to some of the poems. His vision embraces agony and isolation, joy and atonement, celebration, cruelty and magical meaning. Like Seamus Heaney's, his voice is original and compelling, invested as it is with the singing and dancing tones of real poetry.

Age range: 9–18   JO

Themes: Animals, Birds, Birth and Death, Celebration, Violence, Weather

HUGHES, Ted
Three Books: Remains of Elmet; Cave Birds; River
Faber and Faber, 1993
186 pp, paperback, ISBN 0–571–14082–3
Contents, Notes by the poet, no illustrations

Thirty years ago Ted Hughes wrote an introduction to a small book of modern poems called *Here Today*. Stressing the importance of reading poetry aloud he said, 'What matters most, since we are listening to poetry and not to prose, is that we hear the dance and song in the words. The dance and the song engage the deepest roots of our minds, and carry the poet's words down into our depths'.

And what matters most about this new edition from Faber and Faber is that the students encountering it should hear the poems read aloud, and have opportunities to read them to each other. Whether he is dealing with the results of social upheaval, exploring demonic rituals, or communicating his fascination with rivers and fish, Hughes invests his poems with powerful energies and presences. And because they are knitted together in strong, startling patterns his words go down into our depths and allow us to see into the life of things.

Despite some fairly sweeping changes to the book which first appeared as *Remains of Elmet*, and despite the loss of Baskin's marvellous drawings and Fay Godwin's moving photographs, this is a spell-binding collection. One can only hope that examination constraints will not prevent its study by advanced level students.

Age range: 16+   JO

Themes: Arcane ritual, Natural environment, Social history

K

KEMP, Gene
The Mink War
Faber and Faber, 1992
50 pp, paperback, ISBN 0–571–16312–2
b/w line illustrations

The Mink War is Gene Kemp's first narrative poem and is powerfully and effectively written. It tells of a battle between escaped mink and the animals of the wood.

The Mink War escapes the 'tweeness' of many animal, fantasy narratives as the verse is direct and dramatic. No words are wasted to carry the narrative forward swiftly. It includes the themes of man's stupidity and his intervention in the natural order of things, fear, prejudice and hatred (although the outcast, female white rat saves all the animals with her witch-like intervention).

The illustrations by Andrew Davidson are both bold and dramatic and evoke the wood and its inhabitants very successfully.

A book that will be enjoyed by many children both to listen to and to share.
Age range: 7–14   MM
Themes: Battles, Fear, Human behaviour, Prejudice

KING-SMITH, Dick
Jungle Jingles
Transworld (Picture Corgi), 1992
48 pp, paperback, ISBN 0–552–52657–6
Contents, Thematic, colour illustrations

The rhymes about animals in this collection, illustrated in a bright and lively fashion by Jonathan Allen, are great fun to read aloud. Dick King-Smith is never patronising to the young reader and uses difficult and exciting vocabulary – the poem about the elephant contains the words 'indubitably', 'fundamentally' and 'singularly' and children will love to get their tongues around them and work out their meanings.

'Jungle Jingles' looks good enough to entice children and the poems will be enjoyed and quickly learned by heart – especially that real favourite, 'Strippers', a brilliant four-line rhyme about a piranha.
Age range: 4–9   WEC
Theme: Animals

L

LARKIN, Philip
The Whitsun Weddings
Faber and Faber, 1964, first paperback edition 1971
40 pp, paperback, ISBN 0–571–09710–3
Contents, no illustrations

Sharp clarity of thought combine with an almost misleadingly technical ease in this 1964 volume which really assured Larkin's place in English poetry. There has been no erosion by time of his capacity to tease or to touch or, sometimes, to irritate constructively and to raise important questions in seemingly casual, off-hand fashions. Despite a surface prosiness about some of the poems, there is always an underlying, careful crafting of the kind that earns respect and offers useful models.
Age range: 16+   TD
Themes: Common experiences and concerns, Death, Decay, Times past

LEAR, Edward
Illustrated by Louise Voce
The Owl and the Pussy Cat
Walker Books, 1993
28 pp, paperback, ISBN 0–7445–3121–7
Colour illustrations

A brightly illustrated version of the well-loved poem that will really appeal to the very young. The pictures are simple but full of charm and give new life to the familiar characters. The book is well designed with nice touches – such as a small picture of the character who's speaking at the top of each piece of text – that give real clarity to the story.

Age range: 2+   WEC
Themes: Animals, Traditional rhymes

LEAR, Edward and CARROLL, Lewis
Illustrated by Nicki Palin
Owls and Pussy-Cats
Oxford University Press, 1993
64 pp, hardback, ISBN 0–19–276102–1
Contents, Index, Author biographies, colour illustrations

Edward Lear and Lewis Carroll really wanted to make children laugh and their nonsense verse is perhaps still the best around. Anything is possible in their work and some of their crazy imaginings are bound to touch the imaginations of children.

This collection is illustrated in full colour by Nicki Palin and the darker side of the verses is brought out by her rather disturbing, detailed drawings of real people and animals inhabiting strange fantasy worlds. Children will find the words and pictures fascinating but it is more difficult for the adult, who already knows exactly what Jabberwockies, Jumblies and Dongs look like, to accept the new visual images.

Age range: 4–10   WEC
Theme: Nonsense verse

LINDEN, Ann Marie
Steel Drums and other Stories and Poems from around the World
BBC Books, 1992
80 pp, paperback, ISBN 0–563–36375–4
Contents, b/w illustrations

Ann Marie Linden was born in Barbados and now lives in London. The poems and stories in this collection reflect both her worlds. There are the rhythms, heat, colours and exotic fruits of the Caribbean and the markets and seasons of London. There is real warmth in the writing, this is a safe book to smile at and enjoy. Young children will have fun with the counting rhymes that they can chant together to really experience the rhythms.

Age range: 4–7   WEC
Themes: Caribbean, London

LITTLE, Jean
Hey World, Here I Am!
Oxford University Press, 1986
88 pp, hardback, ISBN 0–1927–6082–3
Contents, Introduction, b/w line illustrations

Kate Bloomfield first appeared as a minor character in one of Jean Little's novels, and then as a protagonist in another. She now makes her appearance as a poet, committing her thoughts and ideas, questions and feelings to paper – almost, but not quite, in the form of a young girl's private diary.

Kate writes a lot about the preoccupations of early adolescence reflecting on friendship, parents, old people, presents, clothes, school, being Jewish, writing and the need to write. The pieces, some of which are prose, represent so well the world in which

Kate finds herself. A number of the poems may well lead to discussion and further writing for children in the 10–13 range. Poems like 'Every so often' and 'Working Parents', recognise and investigate the complex nature of family relationships.

Jean Little says that some of the characters in her books seem real to her, and that this is particularly true of Kate. And allowing Kate to 'become' the author, brings to the book a unity and a powerful sense of individuality, which makes this an excellent choice for secondary classrooms.

Age range: 10–13   JO
Theme: Adolescence

M

MACBETH, George
The Story of Daniel
Lutterworth Press, 1986
30 pp, hardback, ISBN 0–7188–2650–7, £8.99
Colour illustrations

Supported by some energetic and colourful artwork by Greenaway Award-winning Pauline Bayna, George Macbeth has largely succeeded in his attempt to put into verse the Biblical story of Daniel. There are some occasional hard-pressed rhymes. From time to time the rhythms sit uncomfortably on the tongue. There is one grammatical oddity (a 'whomsoever' for a 'whosoever'). But, in the main, the story line flows. The poem reads pretty well and convincingly aloud. It will probably be enjoyed by those who read efficiently: it will encourage attentive listening.

Age range: 8–11+   TD
Theme: Bible stories

MacCAIG, Norman
Collected Poems
Chatto & Windus, 1990
456 pp, hardback, ISBN 0–7011–3713–4
Contents, Index, no illustrations

If poetry is that which startles, delights and engages the reader; which reveals and surprises, conceals and confirms; is sometimes wayward, often lucid and occasionally disturbing, then poetry is to be found on every page of this marvellous collection. It is not surprising that Douglas Dunn calls it, 'a wonder book which will give years of pleasure.'

There are nearly 700 poems in the volume, which was published on MacCaig's 80th birthday, and these represent all the published work he wishes to preserve as well as 100 uncollected pieces. All but three of the poems are short pieces dealing with things like bulls, sheep-dipping, herons, a visit to The Uffizi, writers, Brooklyn cops, lovers, the Scottish landscape, blind horses – anything in fact which catches 'the mind behind the eye'. And in 'Writer' MacCaig might well be considering his own position when, having been assailed by poverty and ill-health,

> So far from being silenced
> he wrote more poems than ever
> and all of them different –
> just as a stoned crow

invents ways of flying
it had never thought of before.

What a pity the National Curriculum doesn't require advanced level students to read, declaim, absorb, ponder and delight in the work of a single, major poet like MacCaig, allowing his magic to influence and quicken their lives.

Age range: 16+   JO
Themes: Animals, Love, Landscape, People, Writing

McGOUGH, Roger
Another Custard Pie

Picture Lions, 1993
30 pp, paperback, ISBN 0–00–664351–5
Colour illustrations

A small boy dreams of running away to join a circus, but wakes up to find the circus has left the big-top to spend the day in his house. His amazement grows as he moves from room to room watching the performers presenting their acts. Seals, sword-swallowers, strongmen, alligators and acrobats occupy every available space in the house and eventually the boys' parents are involved:

> Mum on a galloping pony
> Does amazing backward flips
> Dad on a monocycle
> Tries to show off and trips
> (He really should be wearing
> His monocycle clips.)

This is another amusing McGough fantasy, illustrated in colour by Graham Percy. A book for adults to share with small children, or for good young readers to try out on their own.

Age range: 4–6   JO
Theme: Circus

McGOUGH, Roger and RYLANDS, Ljiljana
Noah's Ark

Picture Lions, 1986
34 pp (unnumbered), paperback, ISBN 0–00–663068–5
Colour line illustrations

This lively, irreverent, narrative poem describes the adventures of Noah and the Ark. It is a must for sharing by reading aloud. The humour is quite sophisticated: for example, Noah craftily steers the craft, speaks sternly from the stern; the humour is guaranteed to appeal to most ages. The illustrations by Ljiljana Rylands complement the poem very well; the pigs' worried expression when Mrs Noah speaks of rashers of bacon, the games that are organised for the animals while they are waiting for the raven's return. Some lines, however, hardly need the expertise of an illustrator:

> Then gave it to the air like an unwrapped gift of white paper, that far away glided

when describing the release of the dove.

The strong rhythmic quality of the poem makes reading it aloud equally appropriate for whole classes, groups or pairs. Highly enjoyable.

Age range: 6–12   MM

Theme: Noah

McNAUGHTON, Colin
Who's Been Sleeping in My Porridge?
Walker Books, 1990
92 pp, paperback, ISBN 0–7445–2361–3
Index, colour line illustrations

Colin McNaughton describes this collection as 'a book of daft poems and pictures', but it is really much more than that. The poems are funny, strange, occasionally rude, involving and playful, and the pictures add a wonderful, extra dimension (in colour) to this splendid book.

There are 65 poems in the collection, about giants, aliens, surprising events, pirates, dinosaurs, bogeymen, and twins who are complete opposites. And these, with the help of a number of girls, boys and parents, explore the sort of habits, mannerisms and incidents which appeal to young readers. Great fun, for teachers as well as pupils.

Age range: 7–10   JO

Themes: Aliens, Giants, Dinosaurs, Pirates, Twins

McNAUGHTON, Colin
There's an Awful Lot of Weirdos in our Neighbourhood
Walker Books, 1987, this edition 1992
94 pp, paperback, ISBN 0–7445–1338–3
Index of titles, colour illustrations

Colin McNaughton's prodigious talent enables him to generate genuinely funny, outrageously exuberant verse that gallops along with almost frightening ease. To cap that he has a capacity to match words with art work whose bold grotesqueness constantly amazes and amuses. The humour of text and illustration is bubbling with constant inventiveness – so much so that there are sometimes overspill commentaries on the action embedded within the pictures. It is no surprise that praise of the fullest kind was heaped upon this book on its 1987 appearance. Age has not withered its humour – and it all reads marvellously well aloud.

Age range: 7–12+   TD

Theme: Comic Verse

MacNEICE, Louis
Collected Poems
Faber and Faber, 1966, this edition 1979
575 pp, paperback, ISBN 0–571–11353–2, £12.99
Series: Faber Poets Format, Contents, Index of titles, of first lines, no illustrations

There are 465 poems here – at less than 3 pence per poem – in the Collected Poems of Louis MacNeice, another of the post-1900 poets who disappeared somewhere between the May 1994 SCAA draft proposals for English in the National Curriculum and the DFE's 1995 final version. Clearly in range of themes and moods and in sheer bulk of output, MacNeice is justifiably described as a 20th-century poetic giant. This huge compendium shows him warts and all, able to demonstrate real power even at the end of his comparatively short life. His lyrical skills, his wit, his unending variety make this an invaluable collection.

Age range: 16+   TD

Themes: Childhood, Dreams, Magic, Nostalgia

MAGEE, Wes
The Witch's Brew and other poems
Cambridge University Press, 1989
46 pp, paperback, ISBN 0–521–36941–X
Contents, b/w line illustrations

This is a lively collection of poems for children. The poems cover a wide range of interests; school, witches, Christmas, the weather. Many of them are particularly suitable for chanting out loud, for example 'A Skipping Alphabet' and 'Countdown to the School Bell'. The main ingredient of this Witch's Brew of poems is humour although there is room for reflection and fantasy. The illustrations by Marc Vyvyan-Jones are appropriately fresh and non-conformist; some are an essential feature of the poem, as in 'Climb the Mountain', which is written as a shape poem.

Children will enjoy reading these poems to themselves and sharing them with their friends. Teachers will enjoy these poems too, and not only because many of them provide appropriate models for children's imaginative writing. Poems that play with sounds – the 'S-S-S-Seashore', and 'Puddle and Peel' introduce and use alliteration.

Age range: 6–11   MM
Themes: Fantasy, Humour

MAGEE, Wes
Surprise, Surprise
Longman, 1994
32 pp, paperback, ISBN 0–582–12146–9
Series: The Book Project, colour line illustrations

John rolls out of bed on 1st April and plays tricks on each member of the family in turn. His sister, his dad and his mum are fooled and, as one would expect from a writer as good as Wes Magee, the tricks and their outcomes are inventive and funny.

There is a frenetic pace to the whole escapade, set by the driving beat Magee chooses, and heightened by the wild, wobbly pictures on each page.

Young children will love joining in as they get to know the tale, and will enjoy the ending when John is tricked himself just before noon. Strongly recommended for Nursery/Infant libraries.

Age range: 4–6   JO
Theme: April Fool jokes

MAGEE, Wes
Crazy Cousins
Longman, 1994
32 pp, paperback, ISBN 0–582–12145–0
Series: The Book Project, colour illustrations

This is a brisk narrative poem, bouncing in its rhythms, tidy in its rhymes. It centres on the wet day visit from and play with the three cousins – an improvement in the weather bringing little comfort to Mum. Teddy in the loo and the baby who wants to wee are key aspects of the narrative – all of which is illustrated boisterously by Marc Vyvyan-Jones.

While not essential reading, its commercial intentions never far from the surface, the book would do more good than harm in the young readers' corner.

Age range: 6–7   TD
Theme: Children's play

MAGEE, Wes
Illustrated by Marc Vyvyan-Jones

Missing Bear
Longman, 1994
32 pp, paperback, ISBN 0–582–12144–2
Series: The Book Project, Thematics, colour illustrations

A lively story in rhyme for the very young reader. Teddy bears are always popular and who doesn't know the complete disruption caused in any home when the favourite toy goes missing? Wes Magee's poem has to be read to the end and is well supported by Marc Vyvyan-Jones's more than lively illustrations – very young children will love it!

One of the 'Read-On' books in Longman's Book Project.
Age range: 3–6   WEC
Theme: Lost toys

MAGEE, Wes

Morning Break and other poems
Cambridge University Press, 1989
62 pp, paperback, ISBN 0–521–36940–1
Contents, Thematic, b/w illustrations

A delightful and varied collection of poems about children at school and at home; in fact about growing up. A good book to use to help children to realise that poems can rhyme but don't have to. Wes Magee writes free verse, shape poems and rhymes; he uses a wide range of verse patterns and rhythms and shows the flexibility and scope of poetry. There are many moods in the collection – lots of humour, some fear and touches of real sadness as in 'Until Gran died'. The poems are all carefully observed and have a core of truth which reflects Wes Magee's understanding of children.

The poems are for reading alone, sharing and discussing; together they depict many aspects of children's lives. There are lots of follow-up possibilities in the poet's use of language – such as looking at similes, perhaps starting with,

All day long the sun glared
as fiercely as a cross Headteacher.

Age range: 7–11   WEC
Themes: Growing-up, School

MARE, Walter de la

Peacock Pie
Faber and Faber, 1913, this edition 1988
115 pp, paperback, ISBN 0–571–14963–4
Contents, b/w illustrations

Walter de la Mare is less popular than he was, but there is much in this famous collection that still appeals to children and much for children and adults to read together. Adults will love reading again about those 'Three Jolly Farmers' who bet that they can outdance each other and will still remember 'Some one came knocking' by heart. Poems such as 'Silver', 'Five Eyes' and 'Tired Tim' are just as appealing as they always were.

In this edition Edward Ardizzone's drawings perfectly reflect the mood of the poems and the spirit of the times. Young children will be the richer for experiencing this book.
Age range: 6–10   WEC

MITCHELL, Adrian
The Thirteen Secrets of Poetry
Simon and Schuster, 1993
28 pp, paperback, ISBN 0–7500–1380–X
Introduction: Welcome to Secrets, Conclusion: Extra Secrets, colour illustrations

Adrian Mitchell has written a marvellously funny and instructive book about the magical world of poetry. Each 'secret' is presented first as a tiny poem, thus:

> 'Secret Six'
> Like a poppy field poppy
> Be happy to copy

followed by Tennyson's 'The Owl' which is based on the shape of a Shakespearean song.

There is an immediate warmth about Mitchell's book. His welcome at the beginning of the collection is accessible and amusing. He is one of the great inspirers, pleased to share his passion for poetry with his readers, and anxious to present poetic experience as a joyful gift. He mixes Clare with Lennon and Yeats with Agard in this lovely, wise, easy read which should be compulsory reading for Secretaries of State, Ofsted Inspectors – as well as primary school teachers, parents and the children for whom it will work so well.

Age range: 6–12   JO

MOLE, John
Come on, Wind
Longman, 1994
22 pp, paperback, ISBN 0–582–121930
Series: The Book Project, colour line illustrations

This book is one of the titles in the Longman Book Project, but, like many others in the package, stands perfectly well on its own. John Mole, an accomplished children's poet, imagines a small girl being lifted by the wind and taken on a journey over the town. The results are surprisingly effective.

Simple, direct rhymes and rhythms make this a good book for sharing with very young children. There are lively illustrations to accompany the bouncy text and a satisfying 'return to earth' at the end of the poem.

Age range: 4–6   JO
Theme: Fantasy

MOLE, John
Wake Up
Longman, 1994
22 pp, paperback, ISBN 0–582–12191–4
Series: The Book Project, colour line illustrations

A poem with a simple rhyming structure charts a child's efforts to wake sleeping parents. Although some rhymes may seem unlikely in content from an adult perspective, the simplicity makes it an easy read for young children. Illustrations by Mary Norman capture the light of the early morning and the determination of the parents to stay where they are!

Age range: 4–6   MM
Theme: Waking Up

MOLE, John
Boo to a Goose
Peterloo Poets, 1987
67 pp, paperback, ISBN 0–905291–90–5
Contents, b/w photographs and line illustrations

John Mole has a nimble imagination which is well served by sound, versatile technical control. He writes without any hint of condescension, using a variety of styles. His subjects include riddles, animal songs, amusing rhymes and those poems with a more serious intent. Occasionally he celebrates old fashioned things like penny toys and family games. His voice is engaging, encouraging, sociable. This volume ends with a circus sequence called 'Big Top', which is described as an entertainment for several voices. There are other poems in the collection, like 'Buzz Buzz' and 'Christmas Bells', which would also make excellent group presentation materials.

Boo to a Goose is an accomplished collection of poems by a poet whose work should feature in the curriculum of top junior and lower secondary children everywhere.

Age range: 7–14   JO
Themes: Games, Riddles, Songs

MOLE, John
Water, Water
Longman, 1994
22 pp, paperback, ISBN 0–582–12192–2
Series: The Book Project, colour line illustrations

Enchanting illustrations by Mary Newman match perfectly the exquisitely simple text of this 40-line poem which is organised into ten gently rhymed four-line verses. Risks are taken when such simplicity as this is attempted, but all is rooted in a carefully observed reality of a young child's bath-time that guarantees success. This is bound to be a winner read aloud in the nursery. It will not have lost its appeal with readers of 7 or so. It deserves wider life beyond this particular appearance.

Age range: 3–7+   TD
Theme: Water

MOLE, John
Back by Midnight
Puffin Books, 1994
92 pp, paperback, ISBN 0–14–036657–1
Contents, Index, b/w illustrations

John Mole is an exciting new poet; he won the Signal Award in 1988 for *Boo to a Goose* in which the poems in this light-hearted collection first appeared. There are nonsense poems, rhymes, riddles and knock knock jokes as well as poems such as 'The Regretful Philosopher Apologises to His Cat', about the problems of choosing the right name for a cat, that are clever and thought-provoking. All the poems are well made and can be read again and again. John Mole writes of familiar things and brings them to life with his images and his wit. There's a lot to enjoy and talk about in this collection.

Age range: 8–12   WEC

MOLE, John
The Mad Parrot's Countdown
Peterloo Poets, 1990
50 pp, paperback, ISBN 1–871471–13–3, £4.95
Contents, b/w illustrations

Complemented excellently by Mary Norman's well observed black and white sketchy illustrations, John Mole's 1990 collection of 35 poems confirms the praise he was accorded for his earlier prize-winning *Boo to a Goose*. In a short space, there are remarkable changes of mood from the light-hearted to the gently grave to the almost sombre – and back again. Crafting of a very high order is everywhere evident even in the simplest of the poems. There is something here for all young readers of poetry – but, make no mistake, several of the poems make real demands on thought: they do not patronise.

Age range: 12–16+   TD

Themes: Animals, Ghosts, Riddles, School

MOORE, Marianne
Complete Poems
Faber and Faber, 1968
305 pp, paperback, ISBN 0–571–13306–1
Contents, Index, Notes (35 pp) by the poet, no illustrations

Marianne Moore was 84 when she died in 1972. She was a contemporary of Eliot, Pound and e.e. Cummings. She had a fine eye for detail and a brilliant talent for visionary observation. In her longer version of 'Poetry' she says:

> . . . if you demand on the one hand
> the raw material of poetry in
> all its rawness and
> that which is on the other hand
> genuine, you are interested in poetry

And many of her own poems contain these elements: a fascination with the events, experiences, the encounters of daily routines, and a search for narratives which express them faithfully.

There are extensive notes to accompany the poems. These are placed at the end of the book and the poet suggests that those readers who are annoyed by such detainments should 'take probity on faith and disregard the notes'.

A book for students interested in investigating the complete works of a single and singular poet.

Age range: 16+   JO

MOSES, Brian
Knock Down Ginger
Cambridge University Press, 1994
56 pp, paperback, ISBN 0–521–44683–X
Contents, Notes on planning and carrying out writing activities, b/w line illustrations

Parents, uncles, grandparents, teachers and ancestors jostle with gangs, cow-pats, excavations and donkeys in this busy, bustling collection of poems by Brian Moses. There are poems that rhyme and poems that don't; poems that make you smile and others that make you think; one or two of the poems are unexpected and surprising, inviting a second reading.

At the end of *Knock Down Ginger*, Brian Moses has written nine pages of encouraging advice to the young writer of poetry, suggesting ways in which the poems in this book may be manipulated, managed and modelled to produce new versions. Altogether a very successful venture.

Age range: 8–12   JO
Theme: Animals

MOSES, Brian
Hippopotamus Dancing and other poems
Cambridge University Press, 1994
48 pp, paperback, ISBN 0–521–44684–8
Contents, Ideas for writing, b/w illustrations

Brian Moses's enjoyment of words really shows in this collection and should encourage children to write themselves. He introduces each poem, describes how he came to write it and at the end of the book, offers lots of ideas, addressed directly to the reader, to get children writing. The poems really do offer lots of possible models – there's 'The noisy family rap' which reads aloud so well, many different rhyme schemes, lots of rhythm and onomatopœia – in fact, the young writer is invited to think about words and then to present them in the most appropriate style.

The slightly manic illustrations will appeal to children – they will be happy to pick up this book.

Age range: 7–11   WEC

N

NICHOLS, Grace
Come on into my Tropical Garden
A & C Black, 1988
41 pp, hardback, ISBN 0–7136–2989–4
Contents, Thematic, b/w line illustrations

This is the first collection of poetry by Grace Nichols written specifically for children. The simplicity of style makes them both easy to read and understand for the younger reader while, at the same time, evoking the warmth and sunlight of the Caribbean. Animals and birds are introduced in their natural habitat and a window is provided for observing the life of the people, particularly the children.

The illustrations by Caroline Binch are works of art. They are finely and sensitively detailed and capture the character and life of the poems.

Age range: 7–11   MM
Themes: Animals, Caribbean, Children

NICHOLLS, Judith
Dragonsfire
Faber and Faber, 1990
80 pp, paperback, ISBN 0–571–14373–3
Contents, b/w illustrations

There's lots of variety of style and content in this collection – poems about festivals and about school, about the sea, riddles and beautifully lyrical poems such as 'Dusk'. Young readers will love the teacher/pupil dialogues that are so well observed, the fun of poems such as 'Sloth' in which a sloth has a conversation with Noah, the sensitive and warm description in 'Grandpa' and really the unexpectedness of the collection – there's no guessing about the delight the next page will offer.

The book begins and ends so well and is thoroughly satisfying from the birth of the dragon in 'In the Beginning . . .' to the final poem 'Windsong' –

> I am the seed
> that grew the tree
> that gave the wood
> to fill the book
> with poetry.

These poems will be enjoyed over and over again, they are good to read aloud and discuss and offer interesting starting points for children's writing.

Age range: 8–12   WEC
Theme: Festivals

NICHOLLS, Judith
Wiggle Waggle
Longman, 1994
16 pp, paperback, ISBN 0–582–12131–0
Series: The Book Project, colour line illustrations

A story through rhyme of a caterpillar's journey to butterflyhood. Simple, repetitive language is used effectively and makes this an ideal picture rhyme book for very young children.

Illustrations are equally effective blocks of colour outlined by bold black (rather reminiscent of Dick Bruna) and work well.

Age range: 3–5   MM
Themes: Caterpillar, Growth, Life cycle

NICHOLLS, Judith
Wish You Were Here?
Oxford University Press, 1992
47 pp, paperback, ISBN 0–19–2761110
b/w line illustrations

This is a series of easy to read poems about a family's visit to the sea-side. Although each poem stands by itself, collectively they produce an amusing narrative. There are some well observed touches – Dad's set face and Mum's martyred look ('Family Outing') that most children, and adults, will empathise with. These early descriptions provide the characteristics of the family – Sue's sulks, Pete's indifference. Only Sam, who is seven, thinks that 'sea is heaven'.

As well as the humour there is both sympathy and sensitivity particularly in the portrayal of Grandpa (to whom the book is dedicated).

The book contains humour, adventure and at least one breath-holding incident. The line drawings are light and non-obtrusive.

Age range: 8–14   MM
Themes: Day Out, Sea-side

NICHOLLS, Judith
Illustrated by Lo Cole
Snail Song
Longman, 1994
16 pp, paperback, ISBN 0–582–12130–2
Series: The Book Project, colour illustrations

The text uses repetition, rhyme and rhythm to make a useful book for the beginning reader. Lo Cole's bold illustrations are very attractive and really delight young children. The rhyme is about animals and introduces the words big, small, tall, short, fast and slow. There's no labouring of the points in this book, the text and illustrations carry the early reader through an enjoyable, and most probably a successful experience. One of the 'Read-On' books in Longman's Book Project.

Age range: 3–6   WEC
Theme: Opposites

NICHOLLS, Judith
Storm's Eye
Oxford University Press, 1994
80 pp, paperback, ISBN 0–19–276138–2
Contents, b/w line illustrations

There are some poets writing for children whose work is of such quality that many adults find their poems engaging and worthwhile. Judith Nicholls is such a one, and she rings the bell again with a collection which includes poems as distanced as cockroaches and Cnut; pencils and a Puffing Billy; family trees, starfish and the S.S. *Titanic.*

Such disparate subjects are knitted together with an imaginative eye for detail, a strong feeling for the language of poetry and a transparent love for what she is doing. Nor does she miss the chance to have fun with words:

> Next
> the hexagon
> Here's a perky one
> Six axes of symmetry
> so handy in Geometry
> tessellated simply
> polygon for
> six

Strongly recommended for use with top juniors and lower secondary children.
Age range: 7–12   JO

NICHOLLS, Judith
Midnight Forest with Magic Mirror
Faber and Faber, 1985, this edition 1993
101 pp, paperback, ISBN 0–571–16890–6
Contents, no illustrations

Midnight Forest with Magic Mirror (or *Magic Mirror with Midnight Forest*, depending on which way you hold the book) is two books in one – each beginning at one end of the book and working inwards and, although not a true reflection of each other, there are echoes of poems in each.

There is a wide range of subject matter: events from the Bible (Noah, Moses, the Nativity), poems about spiders, the Rain Forest, school and many more. The poems are simple in form which enables content to be easily assimilated for younger readers. Some are serious in content, others have a much more light-hearted and humorous approach.

It is a useful collection to have in the classroom.

Age range: 7–11   MM

Themes: Bible stories, Family, School

NOYES, Alfred
Illustrated by Charles Keeping
The Highwayman
Oxford University Press, 1981, this issue 1994
32 pp, paperback, ISBN 0–19–272133–X, £3.50
b/w line illustrations

There are those who detest this poem for what they see as its indulging of gratuitous violence. There are others who treasure it as a key memory of their poetry years at school, happy to recall 20, 30 and 40 years later whole chunks of it. In this particular version the drama of Noyes's text is enhanced almost unbelievably by the immaculate skill inherent in Charles Keeping's illustrations. His portrait of Tim, the Ostler, is frighteningly memorable. His shift from photographic positives to ghostly negatives for the two central characters is a touch of genius. It is little wonder that this unique blending of text and illustration is now in its 19th printing since 1981.

Age range: 12–16+   TD

Theme: Love

O

ORAM, Hiawyn
Speaking for Ourselves
Methuen, 1990
63 pp, hardback, ISBN 0–416–15802–1
Contents, b/w illustrations

This volume is described as a Read Aloud book and is written, by Hiawyn Oram, in the voices of three children aged 6, 4 and 1½. The topics cover experiences like falling down, stretching, fair and unfair things, supermarkets, snow and Christmas.

'Doing Things for Myself' deals with the child's desire to be independent and self-sufficient; 'Rare Bear' is an amusing account of a bear repair job that is almost too late. They are representative of those gentle, funny poems which remain true to childhood experience and may well prompt the more sensitive reader/listener to question and reflect.

Age range: 4–6   JO

Theme: Early childhood

ORAM, Hiawyn
Out of the Blue
(Stories and Poems about Colour)
Picture Lions, 1992 (hbk), this edition 1994
64 pp, paperback, ISBN 0–00–664332–9, £4.99
Sectioned by colour, colour illustrations

A dozen or so colours have inspired clusters of stories and poems by Hiawyn Oram, illustrated with his customary panache and wit by David McKee. In all, there are about

110 'items' ranging from four-line poems to 400-word prose narratives. Hiawyn Oram is not the sole author, however, as there are ten acknowledgements also to Shakespeare, Andrew Lang, Alfred Noyes, Anon, Trad *et al*. There are limericks, nursery rhymes, more extended poems, moral tales, and brief observations on aspects of colour. There is much fun; there is froth; there is thought-provoking substance. Occasionally, there is simple fact engagingly presented and especially well illustrated. This is a delightful anthology which has something for all young (and not a few older) readers.

Age range: 8–11+   TD
Theme: Colours

ORME, David
Heroes and Villains
Longman, 1995
47 pp, paperback, ISBN 0–582–12196–5
Series: The Book Project, Contents, Thematic, b/w line illustrations

A collection of poetry which is ideal for reading aloud to and by children, as they all have a very strong rhythmic quality. The title of the book, *Heroes and Villains* is a bit misleading as it is sometimes difficult to sort out who is who – although the children will be able to do so immediately. The majority are very humorous, although contentious; the glorification of a motor bike leaping (over buses) and a speeding lorry driver, for example (who, it must be admitted, gets his just, if gory, desert).

There is a very entertaining word play poem, 'Rough Tough, Brough of Slough' containing the majority of words with the 'ough' letter string. (It rhymes in places.)

Only one poem, 'Sea Rescue', strikes a serious and sombre note. As it stands out from so much irreverent humour it may encourage children to think more carefully about its content.

The illustrations by Lucy Keijser are sparse line drawings and work very well.

Age range: 8–12   MM
Themes: Drivers, Rescue, Traffic

OUSBEY, Jack
Poems from the Sac Magique
Hippo (Scholastic), 1994
62 pp, paperback, ISBN 0–590–55740–8
Contents, b/w line illustrations.

This is a book of rhymes about the characters from Tots TV. Young children will be aware of the characters and the rhymes will link with their experiences. They are simple rhymes to read aloud and share. They have a strong rhythmic quality which almost makes reading aloud essential.

There are lines of French to express a different rhythmic pattern of language, but in a context that gives it meaning.

Good fun – ideal for early learning.

Age range: 2–5   MM
Theme: Tots

OWEN, Gareth
My Granny is a Sumo Wrestler
Young Lions (HarperCollins), 1944
86 pp, paperback, ISBN 0–00–674883–X, £3.50
Contents, b/w illustrations

In a way both title and book cover are misleading, suggesting a diet of comic verse. The reality is different. With discreet support from black and white illustrations by John Bendall-Brunello, the 45 poems in this collection represent a good range of moods, styles, topics, structures. There are tidy four-liners and three-page narratives. Despite a little unevenness in quality, there are more than a few poems here to give pleasure to confident young readers in the later primary/early secondary years.

Age range: 9–12+   TD
Themes: Childhood, Comic verse, Family, Ghosts, Humour

OWEN, Gareth
The Fox on the Roundabout
Collins, 1995
94 pp, hardback, ISBN 0–00–185607–3, £8.99
Contents, Index of first lines, b/w illustrations

There are almost 50 poems here in this pleasant rag-bag of a collection – varying in length from two lines to seven pages. Alongside variation of length there is also variation in mood and tone – from the flippant through to the something quite deep; from the superficial to the gently touching. Teenage love, football, death, the ghostly all find a place – as do Elvis Presley and Georgie Best. Further variations are to be found in the forms chosen by Gareth Owen – from the prosy chat of a poem through to the delicately, traditionally crafted. This is not an all for all collection but there is certainly something for everyone here in the upper reaches of the secondary years (and beyond).

Age range: 13–16   TD

OWEN, Gareth
Song of the City
Young Lions, 1985
94 pp, ISBN 0–00–672410–8
Contents, b/w line illustrations

This is a wonderful collection of poems by a writer who understands children and their concerns as clearly as he knows about poetry and what it can do.

First published in 1985, the characters who engaged our attention then still exert the same power: Sally Ankari; Danny Markey; Bossy Eileen; Grandad Lewis; Miss Creadle, and Anna Mac 'Chip-Shop' O'Sullivan. Teeming with life, bubbling with energy, the poems whisk us into the streets, houses and gardens, building sites and play grounds of the city, sharing with us the excitement of it all.

Some books are worth using until they fall apart. Stuff a copy of this one into your pocket. You never know when you might need to remind yourself, or your class, that life is worth living.

Age range: 9–14   JO

P

PLATH, Sylvia
The Bed Book
Faber and Faber, 1976
30 pp (unnumbered), paperback, ISBN 0–571–14553–1
Thematic, b/w line illustrations

The book is a series of verses about beds! There is a wonderful catalogue of different beds presented in a witty and nonsensical format; jet propelled beds, tank beds for moving and pocket sized beds that only need watering. The joke is consistent. The book should be read at one sitting, preferably aloud. Quentin Blake's illustrations capture the zany humour admirably and also help in sequencing the narrative. A good, 'fun' book.

Age range: 5–15   MM
Theme: Beds

PLATH, Sylvia (edited by Ted HUGHES)
Sylvia Plath: Collected Poems
Faber and Faber, 1981
352 pp, paperback, ISBN 0–571–11838–0
Contents, Index, Introduction by editor, no illustrations

Readers at the top of the secondary school should be introduced to the work of Sylvia Plath and, if they've already met some of her poetry in anthologies, they won't find this book too daunting. It is an impressive collection, full of strength and turmoil and I was forced to remember my own stunned feelings on first reading Sylvia Plath. I turned immediately to 'Daddy' and experienced again that sense of shock I felt when I once heard her reading of the poem on the radio. Sylvia Plath's poetry is full of beautiful lines and phrases that startle and force another reading of the whole piece; they're sometimes breath-takingly powerful and always surprising. Strong stuff, to be introduced with care and sensitivity.

Age range: 15+   WEC
Theme: Family

PRELUTSKY, Jack
Something Big Has Been Here
Mammoth, 1989
160 pp, paperback, ISBN 0–7497–1014–4
Index, b/w illustrations

Along with Shel Silverstein, Prelutsky is one of the best writers of funny verse for young children. He has an imagination which is always fertile and occasionally wonderfully wild:

> Fenton Phlantz is fairly weird
> he puts peanuts in his beard
> elephants are often found
> following Fenton Phlantz around.

Amongst the 200 poems in this collection there are many about children, their habits, concerns and fantasies. Animals both real and imaginary receive the Prelutsky treatment, as do brothers, sisters, puppies and people with weird names.

Something Big has been here is a volume for dipping into and contributes to an important part of the bigger and often more serious world of poetry. Small children will enjoy hearing these read aloud and trying them out for themselves.

Age range: 5–10 JO

Themes: Animals, Family, Fantasy

PRELUTSKY, Jack

It's Halloween

Mammoth, 1978
56 pp, paperback, ISBN 0–7497–0874–3
Contents, Thematic, b/w line illustrations

Prelutsky again! Haunted houses, demons, spirits, games of bob-apple, ghouls and goblins, and skeletons on parade are all present in this jaunty collection of Halloween verse. There is even a countdown poem which begins:

There are ten ghosts in the Pantry,
There are nine upon the stairs,
There are eight ghosts in the attic,
There are seven on the chairs.

If you are looking for tricks and treats, here they are: easy to read poems which will have an instant appeal for the 5–8-year-olds. And the pictures are fun, too.

Age range: 5–8 JO

Theme: Hallowe'en

PRELUTSKY, Jack

The New Kid on the Block

Mammoth, 1986
157 pp, paperback, ISBN 0–7497–0602–3
Index, b/w illustrations

There are more than 100 short poems in this early collection of funny verses by the American writer Jack Prelutsky. The book takes its title from the opening poem which has a most amusing, surprise ending.

A number of poems in this book make enjoyable group presentations – 'Boing, Boing Squeak', 'I'm in a Rotten Mood' – and all are good for reading aloud, simply for fun. *New Kid on the Block*, along with, *Something Big Has Been Here* make excellent, accessible additions to junior libraries. Prelutsky has an unmistakable sense of playfulness – with words, situations, animals and people – and most young children respond well to the anarchic world Prelutsky creates so well.

Age range: 5–10 JO

Theme: Animals

PRELUTSKY, Jack
Illustrated by Arnold Lobel

Nightmares Poems to Trouble your Sleep

A & C Black, 1978
40 pp, hardback, ISBN 0–7136–1861–2
Contents, Thematic, b/w illustrations

This looks just the kind of book that children should enjoy; the spooky black and white pictures have a nightmarish feel to them and certainly fire the imagination. The poems contain lots of shivering, lots of 'gruesome grisly' alliteration but are not quite as frightening and suggestive as the illustrations. There is something rather predictable about Jack Prelutsky's rhyme patterns that seems to lighten the poems and make the reader feel safe rather than terrified of the unexpected.

Although not as menacing as the cover promises, some of these poems read aloud well and some are perfect for children to present with sound effects, or to record on tape – the strong rhythms will teach a lot about using words to create atmosphere.

Age range: 8–13   WEC

Themes: Nightmares, Supernatural

R

RAWNSLEY, Irene

Dog's Dinner

Methuen, 1990

44 pp, hardback, ISBN 0–416–15062–4

Contents, b/w illustrations

Irene Rawnsley is a well-known contributor to many anthologies for young children. In *Dog's Dinner* she presents 30 of her own poems dealing with topics like sausages, caterpillars, wonderful eggs, twin sisters and house ghosts. The title poem is a good example of her work, where a child sleeps in a barley sugar bed and dreams. It has a neat ending and is both inventive and amusing.

The collection is good for reading aloud with catchy rhymes, neat little images and appealing rhythms:

> Poems
> are like tops
> you learn how
> to spin them;
> Words become
> magic circles;
> you hear them
> humming

An excellent addition to the Nursery and Infant poetry collections.

Age range: 4–6   JO

Themes: Animals, Ghosts, Twins

REEVES, James
Illustrated by Emma Chichester Clark

Ragged Robin

Walker Books, 1990

60 pp, hardback, ISBN 0–7445–1108–9

Colour illustrations

In *Ragged Robin* James Reeves takes us on a poetic journey through the alphabet and there are dreams, jokes, descriptions, ballads and other imaginings along the way. The poems are full of rhyme and rhythm; they engage the imaginations of young readers and effortlessly teach a lot about language.

Emma Chichester Clark's illustrations, from the mystery and promise of the endpapers, use colour wonderfully to create a range of moods and take us willingly along this unusual journey. The poems are light-hearted but full of strong visual imagery and, although in some ways they belong to the past, they still have a real sense of magic and offer much to the imaginative child who is already a reader. Wonderful to read aloud and let children simply listen to the sounds of the words and the way they establish atmosphere.

Age range: 4–10   WEC
Theme: Alphabets

RICE, John
Bears Don't Like Bananas
Simon and Schuster, 1991
32 pp, paperback, ISBN 0–7500–0445–2
Contents, Thematic, colour illustrations

A bright and entertaining picture book of poems about a range of subjects including animals, seasons, and the environment. Many are humorous, full of inventive vocabulary, and some have a more serious note. Animal personalities are explored and brought to life – there's the lion with his 'arrogant stare', the rhinoceros 'slow deliberate ponderous – his hammer head lowered in sad anguish', the polar bear a 'pillow on a white sheet' and many more. The collection is complemented by Charles Fuge's bold, colourful illustrations.

Age range: 4–9   WEC
Theme: Animals

ROSEN, Michael
Mind the Gap
Scholastic, 1992
96 pp, paperback, ISBN 0–590–55012–8, £4.99
Index (Alphabetically arranged), b/w illustrations

In a very well presented book illustrated (and decorated) by Caroline Holden, Michael Rosen flexes his prose-poem muscles in now familiar fashion. Young readers with long-developed appetites for his free-ranging iconoclasm will not be disappointed by his output here. They will be provoked and amused. They will also be touched by those few poems which work both directly and indirectly. There is a sense too in which Michael Rosen works hard to make verse easy. In consequence he can overcome some reluctance to the form. (What is less certain is his capacity to develop new poetry appetites – or, rather, appetites for non-Rosenish poetry.)

Age range: 14–16+   TD
Themes: Death, Family, Politics, Race, Relationships, School

ROSEN, Michael
When Did You Last Wash your Feet?
HarperCollins, 1993
94 pp, paperback, ISBN 0–00–672676–3
Series: Lions Poetry, Contents, Thematic, b/w illustrations

Michael Rosen is writing in subversive mood in this collection; many of the poems are funny, but the humour is more cynical than usual and there is more anger. This is a book that will get the most reluctant secondary school children reading. There is much in it for them to laugh at, think about and relate to, for the poet is still very much in touch with the minds of children.

The typographical design of the book gives it a look of today and makes it very accessible and the cover will certainly tempt young readers to look further. Inside, Michael Rosen's poetry is deceptively simple. The hard-hitting lines open up issues of racism and bullying and offer acute memories of school days that are relevant for the present generation. If there are young people who can say 'We didn't used to have POETRY in our class we used to have SPELLING', make sure they get this book so that they can begin to fill the gap for themselves. A book for every secondary school.

Age range: 11+   WEC

Themes: Growing-up, School

Retold by ROSEN, Michael
Illustrated by Helen Oxenbury
We're Going on a Bear Hunt
Walker Books, 1993
36 pp, paperback, ISBN 0–7445–2323–0
Colour illustrations

This re-telling of the well-known rhyme is an absolute winner! Helen Oxenbury's atmospheric illustrations bring the rhythmic text to life. Young children love it, they quickly learn it and join in with the swishy swashy words with their voices and their bodies. The short text is full of onomatopœia and alliteration and introduces the very young to the sound and excitement of language. A great book for the home and for the infant classroom but much older children will also pounce on it like an old friend.

Age range: 2–7   WEC

Theme: Bears

S

SEDGWICK, Fred
Pizza, Curry, Fish and Chips
Longman, 1994
32 pp, paperback, ISBN 0–582–12197–3
Series: The Book Project, colour line illustrations

The 18 poems in this book cover a wide range of topics, some of which explore the episodes and emotions from childhood to adulthood. They evoke the nature of childhood, for example 'The Chatterer', who talks non-stop about a multitude of things; the vivacity of childhood ('Kelly Jane Dancing' and 'Kelly Jane's Bike'), and the longings of adolescence in 'Edward and the Garden'.

Emotions are also explored in terms of memories and reflections, 'A 1914 photograph', in terms of loss and waste. It is difficult to intimate the range of topics without referring to all the poems individually. There should be something to satisfy most tastes and enable children to share and talk about the content and experience of each poem.

The illustrations by Karin Littlewood are lively, colourful and sustain the poems.

Age range: 9–14   MM

Themes: Cats, Children, Dreams

SILVER, Norman
The Walkmen have Landed
Faber and Faber, 1994
85 pp, paperback, ISBN 0–571–17189–3
Contents, no illustrations

The distinctive, sometimes disturbing voice of Norman Silver was first heard in *Words on a Faded T-Shirt*. This new collection is just as compelling, with its investigations into pollution and poverty, computers and trainers, armour, lighting, birth and the problems of growing up in the 1990s.

Silver writes about children's needs, ideas and preoccupations in language that is sharp, well crafted and accessible. He enters their fantasy worlds with an easy confidence. In 'Warrior', the child with a new brace, new shoes and new glasses, uses them to startling effect; in 'Snapshots', thistles and crows, hosepipes and mowers are transformed into magical things; and the puppet in the poem 'Sorry Puppet' is a child who sees himself as a doll that's out of control – a powerful insight into self-recognition.

The Walkmen have Landed is a rich, magical, challenging collection which is never afraid to confront the difficulties and delights of growing up in an unpredictable world. It will be a valuable addition to poetry titles for the later stages of the secondary school.
Age range: 13+   JO
Theme: Adolescence

SILVER, Norman
Words on a Faded T-shirt
Faber and Faber, 1991
73 pp, paperback, ISBN 0–571–16127–8, £4.99
Contents, no illustrations

Thirty-nine poems in a volume described by Matthew Sweeney in the *Daily Telegraph* on its publication as: 'Up front in its concerns, excellent on new relationships, sometimes wittily satirical . . . reality filtered through . . . strangeness, etc.'

Well, there is a range of forms, styles and moods. There is iconoclasm. There is a witty delight in language – but I suspect that the volume will have narrower appeal than Matthew Sweeney imagines. The 'strangeness' he writes of makes for unnecessary obscurity. Moreover, there are aspects which might cause more offence than teachers need to cope with (e.g. 'Bibble' will not delight those with religious sensibilities and references to glue-sniffing, shit, spew, piss, screwing, breasts and caressing bums will not ease teachers' lives). Fewer teenagers will be 'turned on' to poetry by this collection than MS imagines.
Age range: 15–16+   TD
Themes: Modern times, Teenage

STEVENSON, Robert Louis
A Child's Garden of Verses
Brimax Books, 1994
128 pp, hardback, ISBN 1–85854–095–X
Contents, Index of first lines, colour line illustrations

This edition of *A Child's Garden of Verses* was published in 1994, 100 years after the death of Robert Louis Stevenson. They are poems in remembrance of his childhood and reflect the hope, innocence and cheerfulness of that time.

Many of the poems with their frequent mention of 'Nurse' will not have direct relevance for children of today but the emotions expressed may well generate feelings of nostalgia in adult readers about their own childhood.

Some poems, however, are traditional favourites: 'From the Railway Carriage' or 'Windy Nights'.

Mention must be made of the illustrations by Eric Kincaid who has captured the nostalgic quality of the poems. The illustrations are delicately painted and have a misty quality that symbolises time past.

This is a book for any collection and one which will keep children and adults engrossed for some time.

Age range: 6–16+   MM
Themes: Childhood, Nature, Play

STEWART, Pauline
Singing Down The Breadfruit
Red Fox, 1994
80 pp, paperback, ISBN 0–09–928821–4
Contents, Thematic, Index, b/w illustrations

Poetry full of the warmth of the Caribbean and of the journeys and allotments in England. There's a real sense of family in some of the poems and of caring and usually optimism. An interesting range of styles, from the two-liner 'Poor Anancy' to longer verse and conversations, but common throughout is a strong sense of rhythm. This is a good collection of funny and thought-provoking poems – 'Out of Work' is a quite beautiful comment on being unemployed.

Age range: 6–11   WEC
Theme: Caribbean

SWEENEY, Matthew
The Flying Spring Onion
Faber and Faber, 1992
79 pp, paperback, ISBN 0–571–16172–3
Contents, b/w illustrations

Sometimes mysterious, sometimes disturbing, occasionally puzzling, and frequently funny, the poems in *The Flying Spring Onion* are almost sure to stretch the imagination of young readers.

Meet Jan, who lives in a black windmill with a goat he won't name; visit the blue-haired boy who creates havoc in the school dining room; consider the two cows who leave the farm to live on the beach; reflect on the escaped parrot who hops from street lamp to street lamp brightening up the nighttime scene.

Matthew Sweeney's collection is lively, provocative and challenging. There are poems here which will promote debate and encourage discussion in junior and lower secondary classrooms. Sweeney is a regular visitor to schools and it is apparent, at once, that he is well in tune with the preoccupations and interests of young children.

Age range: 10–15   JO
Themes: Childhood, Home, School

T

TENNYSON, Alfred

The Lady of Shalott

Oxford University Press, 1989
32 pp (unnumbered), paperback, ISBN 0–19–272211–5
Sepia and white illustrations

Tennyson's beautiful and powerful poem is presented together with Charles Keeping's illustrations. The page layout is spacious and allows the illustrations full range to complement the poem. They are delicate and sensitively drawn and provide glimpses of country life not viewed by the Lady of Shalott.

It makes the re-reading of Tennyson's poem even more enjoyable in the sense that the book is lovely to look at but it in no way detracts from the emotion and power of the verses.

Age range: 9–18   MM

V

VOCE, Louise

Over in the Meadow
A Counting Rhyme

Walker Books, 1994
28 pp, hardback, ISBN 0–7445–2239–0
Thematic, colour illustrations

This picture book looks good from the endpapers onwards and is lots of fun as animal mothers and their babies leap around making loads of noise in the pictures and in the lively counting rhyme. Children will listen and quickly learn this rhyme and will love doing the quacks, to-whoos, oinks and other animal noises. A good book with large, clear print, it will be enjoyed in the home and in the nursery school.

Age range: 1–6   WEC

Themes: Animals, Counting

W

WADE, Barrie

Rainbow

Oxford University Press, 1995
63 pp, hardback, ISBN 0–19–276124–2
Contents, b/w line illustrations

In Barrie Wade's new collection there are: lullabies and haikus; poems with choruses that rhyme; new versions of old nursery rhymes; poems that don't rhyme where you expect them to; poems that leave the reader to supply a rhyme; poems that march in time but don't rhyme; poems that sing, or snore, or keep on repeating themselves; poems about Suzy Maloozie, Richard of York, Bully Bill McIllican, May Ling and Rashid and Peter; a jostling, bustling, eye-catching, gentle, rumbustious, colourful pot pourri.

That's what *Rainbow* is. Buy it for 7–8–9–10-year-olds. Buy it for 11- and 12-year-olds. And don't forget to sneak a look yourself. Smashing.

Age range: 7–12   JO
Themes: Childhood, School

WADE, Barrie
Barley, Barley

Oxford University Press, 1991
64 pp, hardback, ISBN 0–19–276091–2
Contents, b/w line illustrations

There are two important things to say about this impressive book: Barrie Wade knows about poetry and the way it works, and he has a deep understanding of and sympathy for children.

Barley, Barley contains 63 poems about teenagers, parents, life at home and at school; about the agonies and delights, passions and insights of human experience. The poet recognises the complex situations which confront youngsters in their daily routines and validates their responses without condescension or sentimentality. It is for these reasons that pupils will, in return, respond with warmth to his poems.

Many of the pieces are excellent models for children to use in their own writing. Others raise issues which need to be examined and discussed. And there are those like 'Paperboy', 'Kites' and 'Desert Island' which nudge the imagination and sponsor inner dialogue. Barrie Wade respects his readers, invites them into the world of poetry and shows, rather than tells them how poetry functions.

Age range: 11–16   JO
Theme: Adolescence

WARD, Dave
Candy and Jazzz

Oxford University Press, 1994
64 pp, paperback, ISBN 0–19–276130–7
Contents, b/w illustrations

Candy and Jazzz is divided into three sections – a mixed bag, a group of poems about Candy and her cat Jazzz and poems about the circus. The first section is perhaps the best as it touches on mathematics in 'How many seconds', 'See a Penny' and 'The Biggest Jumper' and goes on to some thought-provoking poems, poems that seem much simpler than they are. And 'The Biggest Joke in the World' is of course not really a joke at all. The poems in the second section touch on everyday ironies and the circus poems show the poet writing with imagination in a very free style.

The most striking thing about these poems is the sense of movement the poet establishes and this makes them read aloud well. This very interesting collection could provide many starting points for discussion on both content and style – 'Dragon Slayer', a very clever poem about smoking, would be a good one to start with.

The poems will be enjoyed by a slightly older readership than the cover and illustrations suggest.

Age range: 8–12   WEC
Theme: Circus

WILLIS, Jeanne

Toffee Pockets: Poems for Children

Red Fox (Random House), 1993
64 pp, paperback, ISBN 0–09–910511–X
Contents, b/w line illustrations

These poems explore the rather special relationship that exists between children and grandparents. They reverberate with warmth and humour and manage to miss the sentimental.

Jeanne Willis captures the child's point of view perfectly; the poems are written in a matter-of-fact tone and the characters she portrays have consistency and constancy, her sister, Chrissie, for example shares in the poems and the illustrations. The illustrations by George Buchanan capture the 'old fashioned' feel to the poem despite the modern context. Like the poems they are full of humour.

A book of poems to be read and enjoyed again and again.

Age range: 6–11   MM
Theme: Grandparents

Y

YOUNG, James

Everyone loves the Moon

Picture Lions, 1991
32 pp (unnumbered), paperback, ISBN 0–00–664096–6
Colour line illustrations

A narrative, early romance poem for the young. It features the courtship of Mr Raccoon and Ms O Possum to the accompaniment of cows crooning and dreaming cats. Mr Raccoon, however, has to overcome the fact that Ms O Possum, like the other animals in the book, only loves the moon. True to form, the romance ends happily with the pair being married beneath the moon.

James Young illustrates his work very well – with muted, moonlight colours.

Age range: 4–6   MM
Theme: Moon

Anthologies

A

ADCOCK, Fleur (editor)
The Faber Book of 20th Century Women's Poetry
Faber and Faber, 1987
330 pp, paperback, ISBN 0–571–13693–1
Contents, Index, Introduction by editor

Fleur Adcock aims 'to show how many good and interesting women poets have been writing in English during the course of this century' and this she surely does. She has selected from the work of poets born before 1945 and has produced a rich anthology of poetry of all kinds with an exciting breadth of style and subject matter. Favourites like Frances Cornford's 'To a Fat Lady Seen from a Train', Stevie Smith's 'Not waving but Drowning' and Jenny Joseph's 'Warning' are included but there are also lots of less well-known poems to discover.

This is very much a grown-up collection but there's much for readers at the top of the secondary school to enjoy too. Just one omission – surely some of the strong black women poets, Maya Angelou for example, were born before 1945 and could have been included.

Age range: 14+   WEC
Theme: Women poets

AGARD, John (editor)
Life Doesn't Frighten Me At All
Heinemann, 1989
96 pp, hardback ISBN 0–434–92523–3, £7.95, paperback ISBN 0–434–92525–X
Contents list of sections, Index of poets, first lines, b/w illustrations

Declaring at the outset his intention to woo teenagers who are allergic to poetry, John Agard sets out a remarkably fresh stall – with writing by teenagers themselves set alongside poetry from around the world. With a strikingly bold, heavily black and white layout, it is the range of voices that gives the book its remarkable quality – the way in which the tight, formal structure of an Elizabeth Jennings poem can stand so close to one by Benjamin Zephaniah. Both are successful in what is clearly a challenging and potentially a rewarding collection. That said, some of the 'newer voices' demand perseverance and it is not a book for those likely to be easily offended.

Age range: 14–16+   TD
Themes: Youth, Teenage, The Body, Love, Racism, School

AGARD, John and NICHOLS, Grace (editors)

A Caribbean Dozen

Walker Books, 1994
93 pp, hardback, ISBN 0–7445–2172–6
Contents, Index, Colour line illustrations

John Agard and Grace Nichols offer a 'mek-up' or 'brata' – an extra bit – a Caribbean dozen of thirteen poets. The poets write a few lines about their childhood and the poems offer vivid recollection of childhood experiences. The poems have a distinctive Caribbean flavour. We read about hurricanes, hummingbirds and markets, but the appeal is definitely universal. They are agelessly topical and fresh.

The illustrations by Cathie Felstead capture the smells, sights and sounds very well in a range of vivid illustrations.

This is definitely a cheering-up book for dull days!

All thirteen poets offer a variety of enjoyable poems. It seems a pity not to mention them all: Valerie Bloom, Faustin Charles, Telcine Turner, David Campbell, Opal Palmer Adisa, Marc Matthews, Dionne Brand, Pamela Mordecai, John Lyons, James Berry and Frank Cellymore as well as John Agard and Grace Nichols. An interesting feature is the Bibliographies of each at the end of the book.

Age range: 9–15   MM
Theme: Caribbean

AGARD, John (collected by)

Poems in my Earphone

Longman, 1995
180 pp, Longman Literature Series, paperback, ISBN 0–582–22587–6
Contents, Index of poets, of first lines, 14 pages of 'activities' designed to promote performance and critical appreciation, b/w illustrations

There are just over 100 poems here well presented in short space and selected carefully for their performance possibilities, those possibilities briskly and helpfully spelled out in a brief section at the end of the book. In addition, John Agard's introduction is dedicated to an account of how he performs some of his own work. There is a truly international flavour to the collection with a mix also of the familiar and the fresh. Attila The Stockbroker is here alongside Auden. There are Hughes and Heaney; Lockhead and Lorca; Carroll, Carver and Causley; Swift and Stevie Smith. About a third of the poems are by women. There is variety here of tone, mood, topic and form. An anthology with practical value and poetic worth, but it is not easy to be specific about an age-group for which the collection is best suited. Some poems have a clearly primary feel: others are more likely, in terms of vocabulary and ideas, to be at home in the upper secondary reaches.

Age range: 13–14+   TD
Themes: Animals, Clothes, Possessions, Furniture, Transport, Race, Computers, Childhood, Adolescence, Environmental issues

ARMSTRONG, Isobel (editor) MANSFIELD, Roger (compiler)

Every Man Will Shout

Oxford University Press, 1964
123 pp, paperback, ISBN 0–19–833145–2
Contents, Index

The editors of the poems in this collection have arranged them on the basis of perceived similarities or contrasts in mood and subject, and each poem, they say, has earned its place because it will illuminate teenage experience.

There are many well-known anthology pieces here – 'Hawk Roosting'; 'Schoolmaster'; 'Welsh Incident'; 'After Apple Picking'; 'Fern Hill'; 'Lessons of War' – and the index is a roll call of well known 20th-century poets. However, more than a third of the poems are written by children and the rationale for including so many is difficult to see.

First published in 1964, the book has had 12 reprints. One wonders why the publishers have not taken the opportunity to represent poetry produced in the last 30 years, particularly by women writers. An anthology intended for use in secondary schools must surely include the work of more than four women poets.

Age range: 11+ JO

B

BACON, Sally (editor)
Chasing the Sun
Simon and Schuster, 1992
95 pp, hardback, ISBN 0–7500–1212–9
Contents, Index of authors, of titles, Foreword, b/w line illustrations

Sally Bacon has compiled a most unusual and stimulating anthology on behalf of The Poetry Society. *Chasing the Sun* circles the globe, picking up poems en route, from places as far apart as Portugal and Antarctica; Afghanistan and Greenland; Alaska and Brazil. There are poems by James Berry, Helen Dunmore, Amryl Johnson, Les Murray and Adrian Mitchell, alongside contributions from the Pueblo Indians, the Inuit, and Chief Bluesnake of the Araucano tribe from Chile. And this diversity carries over into the poem selection – carnival, Yosemite, lions and giraffes, paper-boats, fireworks, mermaids, ceremonial cures – as fact and fiction, legend and reality mingle together.

The royalties from the book go towards furthering the work of the Society in promoting poetry in schools. A good cause, a good anthology, and a good reason for buying a copy for your school library.

Age range: 10–14 JO

BACON, Sally and BLISHEN, Susan (editors)
Ten Bananas More!
Simon and Schuster, 1994
62 pp (unnumbered), ISBN 0–7500–1547–0
Contents, Index, Colour line illustrations

Ten Bananas More! contains poems written by ten contemporary poets, all of whom introduce their own poems.

There is a mixture of humour and seriousness (one or two poems manage both at the same time, for example 'Love a Duck' by Roger McGough) plus a variety of styles, including a Rap ('Baby-K Rap Rhyme' by Grace Nichols). Libby Houston has a wide range of styles and topics in her collection of four poems. 'The Ballad of the Great Bear' tells the story of Zeus, Hera and Kallisto; 'Winter Gnats' has its dancing pattern placed on the page and 'A Maze Dance' is presented in both poetic and visual form.

The anthology contains some powerful poems, two in particular about parents; Brian Patten's 'Little Johnny's Night Visitor' (the fear of a drunken parent) and Jackie Kay's 'Divorce' (of a child from its parents). Adrian Mitchell, James Berry, Philip Gross,

Matthew Sweeney and Helen Dunmore complete the anthology with their collections.

Brian Grimwood uses a very restricted range of colours in his illustrations which heighten their bold and dramatic effect.

Age range: 8–16+   MM
Themes: Parents, School, People, Children, Friends

BAKER, Catherine (editor)

A Brontosaurus Chorus

Mammoth, 1991
61 pp, paperback, ISBN 0–7497–1044–6
Contents, b/w line illustrations

Mammoth Books have a number of humorous titles on their list, by people like Adrian Henri, Jack Prelutsky and Hiawyn Oram. This one contains 24 poems about dinosaurs, some of which are old favourites. Tony Ross's amusing line drawings are great fun.

Like limericks, or old-fashioned monologues, it is easy to overdose on dinosaurs, but small children do find the subject fascinating. Used sparingly, this volume would make a good addition to the shelves of primary school libraries.

Age range: 6–10   JO
Theme: Dinosaurs

BAKER, Catherine (editor)
Illustrated by Chris Riddell

An Armful of Bears

Mammoth, 1994
64 pp, paperback, ISBN 0–7497–1680–0
Contents, Thematic, b/w illustrations

A must for all young bear lovers, this anthology really celebrates bears – teddy bears, polar bears, brown bears, black bears and grizzly bears – bears in their natural environments, not in zoos. There are descriptions, rhymes and story-poems all full of affection and admiration.

Chris Riddell's black and white drawings are very special as he really manages to give all the bears real personality and individuality.

Age range: 4–7   WEC
Theme: Bears

BBC team (editors)

WordPlay; WordPlay 2

BBC Educational Publishing, WordPlay 1992, WordPlay 2 1993
WordPlay, 95 pp, ISBN 0–563–34981–6; WordPlay 2, 85 pp, ISBN 0–563–35390–2
Contents, Thematic, b/w line illustrations

Though these two collections are based on poems used in the BBC series WordPlay, they are genuine compilations in their own right and well worth buying in for Junior libraries.

In the first volume there are poems about friends and families, journeys, letters and animals by well known writers like Gareth Owen, John Agard, Judith Nicholls and Shel Silverstein. And it's good to see the Liverpool poet Matt Simpson chipping in with a group of poems, one of which, 'A Scouser Asks a Question', is a little gem.

WordPlay 2 has a wider selection of poets, including Kit Wright, Wes Magee, Richard Edwards, Brian Patten and Adrian Mitchell. The topics are food, toys, other worlds, tricksters and sports day, and, like those in *WordPlay*, the poems are great fun both for reading aloud, reading for pleasure, and reading to each other.

Age range: 7–11   JO

Themes: Friends, Families, Journeys, Letters, Animals, Food, Toys, Other worlds, Tricksters, Sports Day

BBC team (editors)
Poetry Corner 2
BBC Educational Publishing, 1993
110 pp, paperback, ISBN 0–563–35389–9
Contents, Thematic, b/w illustrations

This is the second collection of poetry from the BBC Schools Radio series Poetry Corner. There are over 200 poems, arranged in 28 loose sections each offering about ten poems on a particular theme – Nearer The Sky, What Am I?, All My Relations, On the Beach, etc. Really, this is an exciting mixed bag; the book is packed with poems of all sorts, old and new, by the famous and the unknown and there is a poem for every young child to enjoy. The lively black and white illustrations on every page help to make this a very accessible collection of poetry.

    A good book for the primary school classroom reading corner, or for the library, offering lots of fun to children dipping into it and reading together.

Age range: 5–10   WEC

Themes: Growing-Up, Myself, Machines, Family, Grants, Holidays, Animals

BBC Publications (Introduction by John Tuckey, BBC Producer)
Verse Universe
BBC Educational Publishing, 1992
138 pp, paperback, ISBN 0–563–34982–4
Series: Verse Universe, Contents, Thematic, b/w line illustrations

Verse Universe is a collection of poems chosen by poets who made the selections for the BBC School Radio series Verse Universe. They have chosen from a range of their own poetry and poetry they like from other writers. The poets, Gareth Owen, Richard Edwards, Roger McGough, Michael Rosen, Benjamin Zephaniah, Libby Houston and the Circus of Poets, are all introduced by a brief biography. Their poems are modern, direct and relevant to children. 'The Commentator' (by Gareth Owen), for example, captures the commentator's style for a street/garden football match, even when describing:

    She's not going to let England have their ball back.

Michael Rosen also chooses children's poems for inclusion in his section.

    Each section is subdivided into themes; an asset for a busy teacher.

    The book is well presented: clear, bold print and a range of illustrators give additional variety.

Age range: 8–14   MM

Themes: School, Football, Friends, Strangers, Animals, Family

BBC Publications (Introduction by John Tuckey, BBC Producer)
Verse Universe 2
BBC Educational Publishing, 1993
143 pp, paperback, ISBN 0–563–35391–0
Series: Verse Universe, Contents, Thematic, b/w line illustrations

This is the second anthology of poems from the BBC series Verse Universe and contains poems that, in general, are more complex and challenging than the first collection. The format remains the same; poems chosen by poets. The poets doing the choosing in this book are John Agard, Brian Morse, Jill and Barry Wilsher and Wes Magee. As might be expected, the choices are wide ranging and include a mixture of traditional (for example, Kipling, de la Mare, Auden) and modern, including the poets themselves! There is the usual mix of nonsense and humour but more deal with issues and concerns. 'Badger' (John Clare) chronicles badger hunting and Gareth Owen's poem relates the agony and anger of 'Arthur, the fat boy'.

Some poems are slightly disturbing in that they explore outside our own world. 'Applemoon' (Rose Flint) for example, relates an incident about an independent shadow. Others reflect the annoyance of growing up ('Dumb insolence', by Adrian Mitchell) and the joys of individuality ('Thumbprint', Eve Merriam).

A full collection, useful for all kinds of poetry-sharing occasions. The contents page, annoyingly, gives poem titles, but not the poet. A minor point.

Age range: 9–14   MM
Themes: Magic, Dreams, Machines

BENNETT, Jill (editor)
A Cup of Starshine
Walker Books, 1991
57 pp, paperback, ISBN 0–7445–3040–7
Index of first lines, of poets, colour line illustrations

Walker Books are always designed and produced with loving care, and this title lives up to expectation. And when a compiler as good as Jill Bennett is working with an illustrator as sensitive as Graham Percy, the publisher's efforts are repaid in full.

Amongst the old favourites in the collection are some new finds: poems that smile and shine out of the pages waiting to be brought to life. If your child hasn't met up with 'Penny Penwarden', 'Sister Jill', or 'The Fish with the Deep Sea Smile', or doesn't know the words of 'Moon-Come-Out', or 'Morning Song', then there is a treat in store for both of you.

It is with complete assurance that this book is recommended to parents, grand-parents, aunts and uncles, friendly neighbours, as well as teachers in Nursery and Infant Schools. Buy your copy now.

Age range: 3–6   JO

BENNETT, Jill (editor)
A Packet of Poems
Oxford University Press,
112 pp, paperback, ISBN 0–19–276066–1
Contents, Index, b/w and colour line illustrations

There have been 15 reprints of Jill Bennett's collection of poems about food, a tribute to the editor's talent for assembling, ordering and serving up the ingredients so well. The poems are split into 'courses' which include, 'specials', mealtimes, snacks, hot-pots and left-overs, and there is a good mixture of old and new poets, seasoned well with 'anonymous' flavours.

Children in the first years of primary school will enjoy the tales of greed, fat ladies, gruesome recipes, the young lad of St Just, and roasted kangaroo.

A Packet of Poems could well be re-labelled, 'A Right Tasty Mix', and, for those who don't already have a copy, a four star recommendation may persuade them to place an order.

Age range: 5–8   JO

BENNETT, Jill (editor)
A Pot of Gold
Corgi, 1993
112 pp, paperback, ISBN 0–552–52590–1
Contents, Index, colour line illustrations

This is a wide-ranging collection of poems 'unearthed' by Jill Bennett. The collection is subdivided into diamonds, nuggets, pearls, emeralds and opals and, although some time could be spent deciding why the individual poems fit into the sections, there certainly are some little treasures to be found. There are poems that will provide a puzzle for children in their meaning and language of poetry ('Who's That?' by James Kirkup, 'Amulet' by Ted Hughes) and others that provide puzzle in riddles. There are counting rhymes, playground rhymes, limericks, nonsense poetry and, unfortunately, one or two bits of doggerel. Some of the poems beg to be read aloud (by children and teachers) for example, 'Brother' (Mary Ann Hoberman). The range of poets includes Tennyson, Ted Hughes, Charles Causley, Mervyn Peake and Michael Rosen.

This is a good collection to have in the classroom and to dip into. The lively illustrations which reflect individual poems are wonderful invitations to the young reader.

Age range: 6–11   MM

Themes: Jewels, Limericks, Counting rhymes, Playground rhymes

BENNETT, Jill (collected by)
People Poems
Oxford University Press, 1990 (hbk), reprint 1992
24 pp, paperback, ISBN 0–19–276110–2
Colour illustrations

There are 12 poems in this slim volume. Nine have appeared elsewhere; the other three are by either Trad or Anon. All are in the comic vein. All are illustrated in extravagant, red-nosed, pantomime fashion by Nick Sharratt. The couple of Causley poems and the single contributions of Roger McGough, Mervyn Peake and Colin West are good to see again, and are likely to bring smiles to the faces of junior school children who hear them or read them for themselves.

Age range: 7–11+   TD

Theme: People

BENNETT, Jill (collected by)
Illustrated by Helen Oxenbury
Tiny Tim
Little Mammoth, 1981, this edition 1993
32 pp, paperback, ISBN 0–7497–0955–3
Colour illustrations

This collaboration featuring Helen Oxenbury's marvellous art-work and Jill Bennett's judiciously loving selection of comic verse for young children won wide and deeply enthusiastic praise on its first appearance in 1991. Reeves and Rosen sit happily alongside Causley, Vachel Lindsay, Trad and Anon in a collection of 20 poems that will continue to give delight for many a year. The artwork is in total harmony with text throughout this most distinguished book.

Age range: 3–7+   TD

BENNETT, Jill (editor)
Illustrated by Ian Beck

Poems for Christmas

Scholastic, 1993
32 pp, paperback, ISBN 0–590–553321–1
Contents, Thematic, colour illustrations

A book full of the promise and excitement of Christmas – the anticipation, the presents, the snow and the real spirit and meaning of the occasion. This is a gentle, happy collection which includes carols, well-known poems like Jean Kenward's, 'Sir Winter' and newer pieces such as Richard Edwards's 'Pilot', which is about that ever-popular wish for a white Christmas.

Ian Beck's illustrations reflect the mood of the poems: the dreamy feel of 'Country Carol', the excitement of 'The Waiting Game', the sense of celebration of 'Kings came riding', the wildness of 'Sir Winter' and on to the calm glory of 'High in the Heaven'. A beautiful book to read, listen to and share.

Age range: 3–9   WEC
Theme: Christmas

Collected by BENNETT, Jill (editor)

Noisy Poems

Oxford University Press, 1989
24 pp, paperback, ISBN 0–19–278219–3
Thematic, Colour illustrations

The twelve poems in this collection are each given a double-page spread and are imaginatively illustrated by Nick Sharratt. They cover a range of subjects – music, weather, food, movement and animal sounds – and are excellent for reading aloud and joining in. The end papers are covered with onomatopœic sound words that really set the scene and get the reader thinking about words and the sounds they make. Some familiar poems but also some new such as the delightful 'Fishes' Evening Song' by Dahlov Ipcar, it begins:

> Flip flop,
> Flip flap,
> Slip slap,
> Lip lap;
> Water sounds,
> Soothing sounds.

The bold, colourful illustrations make the book look inviting and the poems, as well as being lots of fun, will really help young children to develop an ear for language. A book to encourage early enjoyment of poetry.

Age range: 2–8   WEC
Themes: Noise, Sounds

Collected by BENNETT, Jill (editor)

Machine Poems

Oxford University Press, 1993
24 pp, paperback, ISBN 0–19–276114–5
Thematic, Colour illustrations

Another title produced by Jill Bennett and Nick Sharratt in the same style and layout as 'Noisy Poems'. This time the twelve poems are about machines – tractors, washing

machines, cars, trains, phones, hoovers, etc. Again the poems are full of rhythm and onomatopœic words and the illustrations are vivid and humorous and this time the end papers are covered with nuts, bolts and springs. Children will turn to this book again and again.

Age range: 2–8   WEC
Theme: Machines

Collected by BENNETT, Jill (editor)
Tasty Poems
Oxford University Press, 1994
24 pp, paperback, ISBN 0–19–276133–1
Thematic, colour illustrations

The twelve poems in this collection by Jill Bennett and Nick Sharratt are arranged and presented in the style of 'Noisy Poems'. If anything, this book is even more popular with young children. The rhythms and language excitement make the words almost leave the pages. Read it to a child once and be ready to read it again and again. Children will be licking their lips, laughing at 'The wobbling race' and 'Oodles of noodles', tracing the words along the curly straw with a finger and, if they've never tasted a mango, will be insisting that you describe its taste. This time the end papers are gingham table cloths and once again the book looks very tempting.

Age range: 2–8   WEC
Themes: Food, Tastes

BLISHEN, Edward (editor)
Oxford Book of Poetry for Children
Oxford University Press, 1963
167 pp, paperback, ISBN 0–19–276058–0
Contents, Index, Introduction, colour line illustrations

What a pleasure it is to read again Edward Blishen's introduction to this outstanding collection; to hear the wise voice behind the words explaining how poems are 'gathered' and displayed; to sense, once more, his own passion for poetry; and to listen to the reassuring advice he offers: 'Words, lines, whole poems may come to us as mysteries. They may be mysteries that please us, that give us a strange and deep feeling for this or that. And that feeling may be our way of understanding the poem'. Blishen's selection, meant as a sort of introduction to the huge, rich world of poetry, is arranged in sections, each one titled with a poetic phrase. Here are poems that sing, tell stories, chuckle and smile; celebrate tigers and witches and bishops and owls; introduce us to sailors, and good and bad people, as well as calling in major figures in poetry – Blake, Eliot, Hardy, Clare, Keats, Shakespeare, Tennyson and Wordsworth.

Beautifully illustrated in glowing colours by Brian Wildsmith, this is a book which should be available to all children during (and perhaps, even after) their primary years.

Age range: 5–12   JO
Themes: Animals, Poets

BODY, Wendy
Through A Window
Longman, 1995
56 pp, paperback, ISBN 0–582–12240–6
Series: The Book Project, Contents, colour line illustrations and photographs

A collection of poems by women poets which presents different types and moods of poem.

It is a good collection which deals imaginatively with the mundane ('A poem about Housework' by Adèle Geras) and keeps them in perspective ('Family Meals' by Michaela Morgan) while exploring differences. The poems address a range of issues, for example the environment ('Blake's Tyger – revisited', Michaela Morgan), poverty and homelessness, ('Nursery Rhyme, 1992', Moira Andrew) and different countries ('All the way to Africa' by Susan Gates) created by memories and daydreams.

The experiences captured in the book are wide-ranging. It is a very useful collection of new poetry – all the poems are new for the book – which can be used both as enjoyment and stimulus for discussion.

A combination of extremely simple line drawings and brilliantly coloured photographs make the book a visual as well as a poetic pleasure.

Age range: 9–14   MM

Themes: Family, Poverty, School, Environmental issues

BRADMAN, Tony (editor)
A Stack of Story Poems
Corgi, 1992
172 pp, paperback, ISBN 0–552–52709–2
Contents, b/w illustrations

Tony Bradman, a well known children's poet himself, has put together this collection of humorous, narrative poems. There are contributions from Brian Morse, Eric Finney, Gwen Dunn, Wes Magee and the editor himself.

Almost all these story poems have the repetitive, bouncy rhythms of the spoken monologue, with simple rhyme schemes. The most unusual and challenging one, which actually breaks the mould, is Gareth Owen's, 'Benny M'Eever'.

These will be fun for filling in a few minutes during the day, or for entertaining a class during a wet playtime. They need a teacher who enjoys putting on a range of voices and has natural dramatic control. One or two will work well as group presentations and many children will enjoy orchestrating them for such a purpose. Great fun.

Age range: 9–12   JO

BROWN, Marc (collected and illustrated by)
Play Rhymes
HarperCollins Picture Lions, 1992
32 pp, paperback, ISBN 0–00–663754–X
Contents, Music, colour illustrations

A delightful collection of popular play rhymes, illustrated with charm and humour. The actions are clearly shown alongside each rhyme and the music to lots of them is given at the end of the book. Lots of fun for sharing at home or with a group in play group or nursery and infant class.

Age range: 2+   WEC

Theme: Play rhymes

C

CARTER, Ann (Selector)
Illustrated by Reg Cartwright
Birds, Beasts and Fishes
Walker Books, 1991, this edition 1993
63 pp, paperback, ISBN 0–7445–3056–3, £6.99
Index of first lines, Glossary, Colour illustrations

The book cover's claim that 'this is an anthology to treasure' is totally justified – as is the praise received from distinguished reviewing journals on its first appearance. There are Greek and Latin poems (in translation!), poems old and new, light and weighty, from near and far. The illustrations by Reg Cartwright are outstandingly beautiful in their own right, but here confer blessings on sensitively, thoughtfully chosen material. This is indeed a very special book.

Age range: 10–16+   TD
Themes: Animals, Animal conservation

CHICHESTER CLARK, Emma (editor)
I Never Saw A Purple Cow
and Other Nonsense Rhymes
Walker Books, 1990
90 pp, paperback, ISBN 0–7445–3077–6
Index of first lines, colour line illustrations

The authorship of the majority of rhymes in the book is unknown. This is perhaps as well as the book is, as the sub-title suggests, full of nonsense. Even the attributable poems (Lear, Carroll, Belloc and Goodrich) are nonsensical in the extreme. Young children will love them. There are mixed-up nursery rhymes with characters appearing in rhymes where they should not be, limericks, tongue-twisters, even rhymes with au pairs. In all there are 117 rhymes, all of which feature animals, including the purple cow.

Every rhyme is illustrated by Emma Chichester Clark, a beautiful, old-fashioned accompaniment that complements the words.

Age range: 4–8   MM
Theme: Animals

COHEN, Mark (editor)
Cohen's Cornucopia
Patrick Hardy Books, 1983
112 pp, hardback, ISBN 0–7444–0001–5
Contents, b/w line illustrations

A collection of tongue-twisters that range from one-liners; 'Old, oily ollie oils oily autos' to 8 pages of cumulative verse. Many are old favourites, some are in French (or Spanish or Italian) and others are published verse ('The Modern Major General', W.S. Gilbert, Michael Rosen, for example). A book to dip into and find particular favourites. Most *have* to be read aloud – it adds to the fun. A good book to have in the classroom although teachers will need to practise their reading aloud! Amusingly illustrated by Colin West.

Age range: 7–14   MM
Theme: Tongue-twisters

COLE, William (editor)
Illustrated by Tomi Ungerer

Oh, That's Ridiculous!

Mammoth, 1991
96 pp, paperback, ISBN 0–7497–0584–1
Contents, Thematic, Index, b/w illustrations

This anthology will really appeal to children who love the ridiculous and it is a good one for those who are reluctant to pick up a poetry book. The fun and positive experience it offers may well offer children a way into poetry. The poems are presented in an uncrowded way and the illustrations are hilarious. The book introduces that famous 'Young Lady of Spain', warns against getting rain in the head, introduces the cautionary tale – this one is of 'Godfrey Gordon Gustavus Gore – No doubt you have heard the name before – Was a boy who never would shut a door!', and generally offers lots of fun and nonsense. A useful anthology for any book corner.

Age range: 7–12   WEC
Theme: Ridiculous, The

COLE, William (selected by)

Oh, How Silly!

Mammoth (Mandarin Imprint), 1971, re-issued 1975 & 1991
94 pp, paperback, ISBN 0–7497–0583, £2.50
Contents, Index of authors, of titles, b/w illustrations

Nearly 25 years old now, this collection of 55 nonsense poems (and songs) contains examples by familiar names in this territory – such as Silverstein, Milligan, Nash, Prelutsky, Belloc and Graham – as well as less familiar names and one or two Anons. William Cole's own introductory poem hopes that the collection will amuse – and it does that, helped in its rôle by some simple, clever illustrations by Tomi Ungerer. More than a few smiles can still be raised by this high-spirited collection.

Age range: 8–13+   TD
Themes: Humour, Nonsense

COOK, Helen and STYLES, Morag (editors)

Dream Time

Cambridge University Press, 1991
32 pp, paperback, ISBN 0–521–39954–8
Contents, Thematic, b/w and colour illustrations

The poems in this collection are about the magic of dreams, night dreams and day dreams, the times when you're living alone in your head apart from the rest of the world. There are some haunting lines, that lovely word 'gloaming' in a poem by Walter de la Mare, loneliness in Roger McGough's 'Bully Night' and extracts from those magical texts, 'Alice in Wonderland' and 'The Tempest'. A sensitive collection to read and discuss from W.H. Auden's piece on the first page:

> Since he weighs nothing,
> Even the stoutest dreamer
> Can fly without wings.

to 'Shepherd's Night Count', by Jane Yolen, on the last page.

Age range: 6–12   WEC
Theme: Dreams

COOK, Helen and STYLES, Morag (editors)
Take Me Like I Am
Cambridge University Press, 1991
32 pp, paperback, ISBN 0–521–39960–2
Series: Cambridge Poetry Box, Contents, Thematic, b/w and colour illustrations

This is a slim collection of poems (22) that explores the individuality of the person and celebrates that individuality. Additionally the uncertainties and loneliness of the young are addressed by the poets who include Michael Rosen, Adrian Mitchell, Wes Magee and William Blake. Phoebe Hesketh describes the delight of knowing children like 'Sally' who are full of inconsistencies of behaviour. Younger readers will have few problems identifying with the themes that are expressed. The illustrations by Carey Bennett, some in black and white, others in rich colour, capture the ideas expressed verbally and further enhance the quality of this delightful collection.

Age range: 7–15   MM
Themes: Individuality, People

COOK, Helen and STYLES, Morag (editors)
Bananas in Pyjamas
Cambridge University Press, 1991
32 pp, paperback, ISBN 0–521–39948–3
Series: Cambridge Poetry Box 1, Contents, b/w and colour line illustrations

A collection of rhymes for amusement. It incorporates skipping and playground rhymes with verse from Lewis Carroll ('Twinkle Twinkle Little Bat') Lear, Spike Milligan and Michael Rosen to name but a few. No seriousness here! The illustrations, some black and white, some in colour, by Jane Gedye are delightfully matter of fact and capture much of the idiocy perfectly. Young children will enjoy this book.

Age range: 6–9   MM

COOK, Helen and STYLES, Morag (editors)
Don't Do That!
Cambridge University Press, 1991
32 pp, paperback, ISBN 0–521–39952–1
Series: Cambridge Poetry Box 1, Contents, Thematic, b/w and colour illustrations

There's so much in this slim collection for children to relate to and it certainly makes one wonder how anyone actually survives childhood! All those 'don'ts' that parents are so fond of are here as remembered (probably) by such poets as Michael Rosen, John Agard and Wendy Cope. The feeling of the anthology can be summed up by the closing words of Spike Milligan's 'Kids' – 'Why do you keep on having us?' Children will love this book and will be encouraged to write of their own similar experiences. The poems are so varied in style and language that one of them is bound to touch every young reader.

Age range: 5–11   WEC
Themes: Childhood, Children and Parents

COOK, Helen and STYLES, Morag (editors)
Pussy Cat, Pussy Cat
Cambridge University Press, 1991
32 pp, paperback, ISBN 0–521–59946–7
Series: Cambridge Poetry Box 1, Contents, b/w and colour illustrations

With a mix of black and white and colour illustrations by Penelope Taylor, of generally sound and supportive quality, this is a selection of 25 poems (or extracts from longer ones) by poets old and newish – including two poems by children and a couple of 'traditionals'. There's Milligan, Farjeon, Blake, McGough, Kit Wright and Mick Gowar – and others, all rarely represented by more than a dozen lines or so. Apart from the children's poems, there's nothing of very recent vintage. That said, there is variety of mood and style here and enough of quality to win poetry friends in the 6–12 age group.

Age range: 6–12   TD
Theme: Cats

COOK, Helen and STYLES, Morag (editors)
My Brother's A Beast
Cambridge University Press, 1991
32 pp, paperback, ISBN 0–521–39950–5
Series: Cambridge Poetry Box 2, Contents, b/w and colour line illustrations

Another Cambridge Poetry Box Selection from Helen Cook and Morag Styles, put together with the kind of imaginative grasp one comes to expect from two such experienced compilers.

Young children will love the family stories, told in a range of contemporary voices and well illustrated by Michael Charlton. Wes Magee, Kit Wright, John Agard, James Berry, Michael Rosen they are all winners in this little book which is just right for 6–9-year-olds.

Age range: 6–9   JO
Theme: Family

COOK, Helen and STYLES, Morag (selected by)
It's a Mad, Mad World
Cambridge University Press, 1991
32 pp, paperback, ISBN 0–521–39958–0
Series: Cambridge Poetry Box 3, Contents, b/w and colour illustrations

There are 25 short poems in this slim volume, all benefiting from the stylistic range of black and white and colour illustrations by Caroline Holden. The two traditional and one anonymous poems are embedded in poems by British, Japanese, Czech, Caribbean and American writers. There is an emphasis on the brief, poems ranging from three to about 25 lines. Variety of shape and style is apparent in a selection which, like others in the series, is likely to have beneficial appeal. There is also a shifting of mood from the broadly comic to the gently lyrical to the neatly savage that makes for likely success.

Age range: 10–12+   TD
Themes: Animal rights, Humour, Natural World, Nonsense

COOK, Helen and STYLES, Morag (editors)
By the Pricking of My Thumbs
Cambridge University Press, 1991
32 pp, paperback, ISBN 0–521–39956–4
Series: Cambridge Poetry Box 2, Contents, b/w and colour illustrations

Spells, phantoms, water sprites, witches and a Frozen Man feature in this collection of spooky poems in the Cambridge Poetry Box series. Helen Cook and Morag Styles are accomplished anthologists and the twenty-one selected poems fit well together to provide a satisfying mixture of old and new.

A traditional Gaelic omen, extracts from *Macbeth*, and a charm by Ben Jonson sit nicely alongside contributions from Kit Wright, John Agard and Charles Causley. Rose Flint's 'Applemoon' is an atmospheric piece which may well prickle the reader's skin, and it is good to see a puzzling little mystery by Miroslav Holub at the end of the collection.

Age range: 6–9   JO

Themes: Ghosts and witches, Spells and charms

COOK, Helen and STYLES, Morag (editors)
Come Rock with I

Cambridge University Press, 1991

32 pp, paperback, ISBN 0–521–39962–9

Series: Cambridge Poetry Box 3, Contents, colour illustrations

With the support of lush colour illustrations by Tamara Capellaro, several of the 22 short poems in this little 'series' book are by black writers from Afro-Caribbean or American backgrounds. There is throughout a strong emphasis on the rhythms of dance and song – with occasional hints of rap, the most successful in this latter vein being 9-year-old Kuntiss Horswell's amusing contribution. To get the most out of some of these poems, one needs to hear them read (or sung) aloud by authentic voices. That said, there is much here to open eyes and delight ears.

Age range: 10–12+   TD

Themes: Dancing, Songs

COPE, Wendy (editor)
Is that the New Moon?

Lions (HarperCollins), 1993

126 pp, paperback, ISBN 0–00–673240–2

Contents, Index of authors, b/w line illustrations

Wendy Cope has gathered together a collection of poems by women, about women and, originally, for young women aged 13–16 years. Such a wealth of poetical experience however should not be confined to a particular age range or gender; the potential appreciative audience is far wider.

The poets, most living, most based in the UK (although origins differ and are reflected in their poems), write about their own and others' experience. The poems traverse a gamut of emotions; sad, happy, uncertain, loving, reflective and mirror, enhance and extend the reader's own perceptions and experience. They are all accessible to the reader (a criterion for selection), in content and meaning. This is a collection that will be enjoyed. Wendy Cope, in her introduction, states that she hopes it will be an introduction for many to the enjoyment of poetry. I think she will be proved right.

Modern, unsentimental illustrations by Christine Roche accompany the majority of the poems.

Age range: 13–16+   MM

Theme: Women

CROSS, Vince (editor)
Illustrated by Nick Sharratt
Sing a Song of Sixpence – popular nursery rhymes

Oxford University Press, 1994

32 pp, paperback, ISBN 0–19–272272–7

Colour illustrations

An exuberant collection of well-loved nursery rhymes and songs, given new life by amusing and colourful illustrations. The pictures are well worth looking at and discussing. Is that Johnny coming from the fair hand-in-hand with another girl – and without the 'bunch of blue ribbons' he'd promised another? That's just one of the many questions/observations made by a group of four-year-olds.

The book is a good introduction to nursery rhyme for very young children who always respond with enthusiasm to Nick Sharratt's distinctive illustrations.

Age range: 2–6   WEC

Theme: Nursery rhymes

CURRY, Jennifer (editor)

The Best of Children's Poetry

Red Fox, 1993
235 pp, paperback, ISBN 0–09–918191–6
Contents, Index, Foreword, b/w line illustrations

Jennifer Curry has selected some of the best poems from the Cadbury's National Exhibition Competition, first held in 1983. The contributors' ages range from four to seventeen and the editor has chosen poems by working to her own set of criteria. She has looked for a genuine child's eye view of the world, and taken into account originality, freshness, humour, clarity, and the competency exercised in using form and structure. The poems are divided into eleven sections, with a single poem to open and close the book.

There are some delightful pieces of work here which will provide fascinating reading for children of all ages. This is the kind of book teachers should have available to dip into and share, whenever there is an odd moment to be filled. Then leave a copy around so that children can browse and pass their findings on to friends.

Age range: 5–16   JO

CURRY, Jennifer (editor)

The Last Rabbit

Mammoth, 1992 (First published Methuen, 1990)
109 pp, paperback, ISBN 0–7497–0252–4, £2.99
Contents, Index of poets, of first lines, a few b/w illustrations at heads of sections only

In its sixth printing since its first appearance in 1990, this is a weighty little selection of over 80 poems, all centred on nature and animals – with very much a conservationist aim in mind. Winning the 1991 Earthworm Award, the book includes traditional and modern verse on this theme – the familiar and the fresh – with some striking pieces by children and young people. Crusading energy sits confidently alongside the more calmly lyrical, making for an anthology that deserves to have a keen, wide audience. Young readers' language storehouse can only be enriched by the range here of style and image.

Age range: 11–16+   TD

Themes: Animals, Conservation, Nature

CURRY, Jennifer (editor)

Scrumdiddly

Red Fox, 1993
96 pp, paperback, ISBN 0–09–995100–2
Thematic, Index of first lines, b/w line illustrations

Scrumdiddly is a collection of rhymes and poems about food.

The great majority are humorous and entertaining, ideas to nibble at at odd times in the classroom. There are some poems, however, that offer more challenge in terms of images and response, for example, 'Wild Strawberries' (Leonard Clark) and 'Souldern Christmas Feast' (Jennifer Curry). These poems will be re-read not only for their superficial enjoyment but to explore the juxtaposition of the words and to savour their rhythm.

An enjoyable collection for the classroom; many of the poems will be shared and repeated endlessly!

Illustrations by Susie Jenkin-Pearce add their own dimension and humour to the poems.

Age range: 8–13   MM

Themes: Tastes, Food

CURRY, Jennifer (editor)
Them and Us – Pairs of poems for young and old
Red Fox (Random House), 1994
96 pp, paperback, ISBN 0–09–995110–X
Contents, Thematic, Index, b/w line illustrations

This is an interesting juxtaposition of young (2½–15 years) poets and more established writers. Each double-page spread has a particular topic, for example, 'falling in love' or 'rage' with two poems; one written by the young poet and the other by the adult poet. It works very well. The poems are usually written from the perspective of the child or adult and the combination of the two gives clarity, depth and greater insight into the topic being explored. The youngest poet's (2 years 4 months) contribution (scribed by his father) is about making a snowman and is delightful: 'I will make a snow hand And hold it'. Many of the more established poets will do well to look over their shoulders at the talent of younger writers that is prevalent in this book.

This is a successful anthology which explores a whole range of emotions.

Illustrations by Susie Jenkin-Pearce are unobtrusive and complement the poems.

Age range: 4–16   MM

Theme: Young and old

CURRY, Jennifer (editor)
In Love: a collection of love poems
Teens – Mandarin, 1991
138 pp, paperback, ISBN 0–7497–0251–6
Contents, Index

Jennifer Curry's collection of love poems is rather odd in some of its choices but that does not detract from the overall quality of the book. It has the range from traditional to modern (Shakespeare, Sidney, Browning to Larkin, Mitchell and McGough). Many of the poems are absolutely up to date. 'First Ice' by Audrey Voznesensky, for example, tells of a girl's hurt via the telephone wires in a draughty telephone kiosk.

Some of the poets are also ultra-modern; the youngest is 9 ('Lovely Tracy' by David Phipps). The others are 14–17 and all write about their experiences of love. It is refreshing to read young love poetry from both sexes; love and poetry are alive and well.

Overall it is a rich and varied collection and covers the range of love: early love, first love, lost love, weddings and happy endings. A poem, in fact, for every occasion.

The variety of styles will ensure that at least some poems will appeal to everyone.

Age range: 10–16+   MM

Theme: Love

CURRY, Jennifer (editor)
Dove on the Roof
Mammoth, 1992
110 pp, paperback, ISBN 0–7497–1056–X, £2.99
Contents, Index of poets, of first lines

There are almost 80 poems in this slim paperback presented virtually without illustration. They include extracts from the Bible and from Shakespeare, poems by children, by Hardy, Auden, Sassoon, poems of very recent making. The quality of the verse is, perhaps, inevitably uneven – especially given the fact that the child contributors (and probably several of the adults) are writing beyond their experience. That said, there is an urgency about the innocence of the young, a touching quality to their protestations. When these are set alongside the perceptions of adults the result is an anthology that is never less than interesting. It must make food for thought, talk and further reading – and writing. It is important to note, moreover, that there are some lighter touches.

Age range: 10–14+   TD
Themes: Childhood, War

D

DAVEY, Gwenda Beed (editor)
Jack and Jill: A Book of Nursery Rhymes
Oxford University Press, 1993
67 pp, hardback, ISBN 0–19–553318–6
Index, colour line illustrations

First published in 1966, *The Mother Goose Treasury* is the one against which all collections of nursery rhymes will be measured. This publication, compiled by Gwenda Beed Davey, is based on research to determine which rhymes are the most popular with parents and children. It is, therefore, more modest in its scope than the Raymond Briggs classic, but is a bright, lively collection, beautifully produced by OUP with an appropriate range of detailed, full colour illustrations.

Observant children may notice that the people in the illustrations all look as though they belong to the same family – apart from Michael Finnegan, that is – with pert, turned up noses and rose-bud mouths.

Age range: 2–5   JO

F

FISHER, Robert (editor)
Minibeasts, A Book of Poems
Faber and Faber, 1992
72 pp, paperback, ISBN 0–571–17159–1
Contents, b/w line illustrations

This time Robert Fisher has collected poetry about tiny creatures both pleasant and unpleasant. The unpleasant appeal enormously to young readers – they will enjoy such poems as 'Ants, although Admirable, Are Awfully Aggravating', 'Earwig O!' and those about fleas and bedbugs. But the beautiful haikus translated from the Japanese offering pictures of butterflies and dragonflies will also delight and will teach a lot about economy of language.

The illustrations, by Kay Widdowson, particularly the one of the scorpion in bed, add humour and help to bring the poems to life.

Age range: 7–12   WEC

Themes: Insects, Minibeasts

FISHER, Robert (editor)

Pet Poems

Faber and Faber, 1989

89 pp, paperback, ISBN 0–571–16830–2

Contents, b/w line illustrations

Robert Fisher has collected together a rich variety of poems about pets usual and unusual, serious and light-hearted, by children and by established poets. The mood and style vary from page to page; we have a shaggy dog, a dog with fleas, a hairy dog, a sleepy dog, an adventurous dog, a Best Friend, a dream of a dog and the dog not wanted once the excitement of the Christmas present has faded. Then there are cats and less usual pets such as a hippopotamus, a yak and a bull – the bull is in a poem from Africa and is much more than a pet.

The book raises big issues such as dealing with death, animal freedom and the whole idea of turning animals into pets. An interesting, thought-provoking collection of poetry written in many forms.

Age range: 7–12   WEC

Themes: Animals, Pets

FOREMAN, Michael (illustrator)

Mother Goose

Walker Books, 1991

160 pp, hardback, ISBN 0–7445–0775–8

Index, Foreword, colour line illustrations

A brilliant collection of over two hundred traditional rhymes, rhymes that Iona Opie calls in her Foreword 'the first furnishings of the mind', illustrated with great style and imagination by Michael Foreman. The rhymes are loosely linked by theme and are linked on each double page by the illustrations. The pictures often link the pages too – Mary's lamb has walked over into that other Mary's garden, Humpty Dumpty's legs are in the air on the page before his story appears and the Duke of York's men begin to march at the end of Humpty Dumpty's page! A book to share and look at very carefully as it offers rhymes for all moods. It ends peacefully with three double pages of lullabies set against a background of Michael Foreman's stunning blue.

Age range: 1–7   WEC

Themes: Nursery rhymes, Traditional rhymes

FOSTER, John (compiler)

A Very First Poetry Book

Oxford University Press, first published 1984, this reprint 1994

128 pp, hardback ISBN 0–19–916051–1, paperback, ISBN 0–19–916050–3, £3.50

Contents, Index of first lines, colour and b/w line illustrations

This is a deservedly popular anthology – as its 6 hardback and 12 paperback reprintings make plain. There are 102 poems – very good value for money – by poets well established and poets less well known. The emphasis is largely upon the light, but there are some more seriously intentioned pieces. For some adults, the clash of styles in the work of the three illustrators may be a little hard to take. On the other hand, less prejudiced child eyes seem to find that matter less problematic.

> This is a book likely to give young children an excellent start on their poetry journeys.
> Age range: 4–8+   TD
> Themes: Animals, Childhood

FOSTER, John (compiler)
Another Very First Poetry Book
Oxford University Press, first published 1992, this reprint 1994
96 pp, hardback ISBN 0–19–917209–0, paperback, ISBN 0–19–917209–9, £3.50
Contents, Index of first lines, colour line illustrations

Altogether this anthology has had five printings since its first appearance in 1992. It follows the same format as the 11 others in the series. The verse, largely rhymed, generally has a focus on the interests and concerns of young children. The emphasis is light rather than weighty. The clear aim is to delight the young and to draw them painlessly into the world of verse. Although there continue to be some reservations about the vivid contrasts in illustrative style – there are six artists at work here – there is no doubt that the book deserves a firm primary school place.

> Age range: 4–8+   TD
> Themes: Animals, Childhood, Family, Play

FOSTER, John (editor)
A First Poetry Book
Oxford University Press, first published 1979, this reprint 1994
128 pp, hardback ISBN 0–19–918113–6, paperback, ISBN 0–19–918112–8
Contents, Index of first lines, colour and b/w line illustrations

Emerging now in its 16th paperback edition with 14 hardback printings also to its credit, this is, in fact, the first in the John Foster Oxford Poetry Book Series. The pattern of a variety of illustrative hands is established here – the softer, gentler, less-comic artwork generally more appealing and more successful. The proof of the poetic pudding is, however, clearly, in the poetic eating of reprints. A careful editorial hand has been at work here to ensure an excellent range of styles, forms and moods generally in these 100 or so poems by writers well-established or hitherto unknown. There is something here to appeal to every child – as listener or as reader.

> Age range: 7–10+   TD
> Themes: Animals, Childhood, The Elements, Seasons

FOSTER, John (editor)
Another First Poetry Book
Oxford University Press, first published 1987, this reprint 1993
128 pp, hardback ISBN 0–19–917120–3, paperback, ISBN 0–19–917119–X, £3.50
Contents, Index of first lines, colour and b/w line illustrations

Together, the hard and paperback editions of this volume in this extensive series have seen a total of seven printings. Although five illustrators seek here to complement the written word, there are fewer extreme clashes of style in this particular volume than in some of the others. As far as the verse is concerned, John Foster's touch continues to be remarkably assured in his selection of over 110 poems; somewhere near a third of them appears in print for the first time. He has provided again a mix of moods, a range of styles and a variety of poetic language and image which can only be of benefit to young children who meet the book.

> Age range: 7–10+   TD
> Themes: Animals, Childhood, Family, Nature, School

FOSTER, John (editor)

A Second Poetry Book

Oxford University Press, first published 1980, this reprint 1993
126 pp, hardback ISBN 0–19–918137–3, paperback, ISBN 0–19–918136–5, £3.50
Contents, Index of first lines, colour and b/w line illustrations

One of the earlier books to emerge in this series of 11, this features the work of four artists' illustrations of about 100 poems, the clash of styles perhaps more irritating to an adult's than to a child's eye, the adult perhaps also less patient with the brasher cartoonery. That reservation apart, it is impossible to fall out with John Foster's selection. There is, again, an excellent variety of material here – something to speak to and happily influence every reading child. Short and snappy, wise and witty, delicate and rumbustious are to be found here – established and new poets sitting comfortably alongside each other. (Forgivable here, as it is one of the earliest in the series, is the failure to ensure a better reflection of our multi-cultural society in the illustrations – a fault well rectified in later appearing volumes.)

Age range: 8–12+   TD

Themes: Animals, Childhood, Family, Nature, School

FOSTER, John (editor)

Another Second Poetry Book

Oxford University Press, first published 1988, this reprint 1993
127 pp, hardback ISBN 0–19–917122–X, paperback, ISBN 0–19–917121–1, £3.50
Contents, Index of first lines, colour and b/w line illustrations, colour photographs

About a third of the 100 plus poems in this volume are appearing for the first time in print with eight contributions at least from poets of Caribbean origin. That said, ethnic minority figures make few appearances in the illustrations which come from ten different hands. In verse terms, this volume, however, upholds the traditions John Foster has sought to establish in the series as a whole. Trivialities that are designed to do little (if anything) more than amuse are set beside more thoughtfully earnest material. There is something for every poetic taste – and something to establish new tastes too. About the whole collection there is a kind of *joie de vivre* that argucs for its firm place in primary and secondary school libraries.

Age range: 8–12+   TD

Themes: Animals, Childhood, Family, Nature, School, Seasons

FOSTER, John (editor)

A Third Poetry Book

Oxford University Press, first published 1982, this reprint 1994
126 pp, paperback, ISBN 0–19–918139–X, £3.50
Contents, Index of first lines, colour and b/w line illustrations, b/w photographs

Now in its twelfth printing, this selection again has something in the region of a third of its 100 or so poems appearing in print for the first time – with only 3 illustrators at work to support the text. Some of the best known names in the children's poetry field are well-represented here – Wes Magee, Max Fatchen, Gareth Owen, Judith Thurman, Kit Wright, Charles Causley – to name invidiously but a few. And there are some newer names with bright contributions on show. Young readers will take comfort from an acquaintance with the familiar format of this series. They will know there is something in here to suit every taste and every mood. No wonder this volume is already in the twelfth printing.

Age range: 10–13+   TD

Themes: Animals, Childhood, Family, Seasons

FOSTER, John (editor)

Another Third Poetry Book

Oxford University Press, first published 1988, this reprint 1994
128 pp, paperback, ISBN 0–19–917123–8, £3.50
Contents, Index of first lines, colour and b/w line illustrations, colour and b/w photographs

There are over 100 poems in this selection, almost a third of them appear for the first time. The popularity of the book is signalled by the fact that this is its sixth printing. It is difficult to know what new to say about the product of such a fecund anthologist. Once again, he has employed a host of illustrators – nine this time – and they have served well both the poets' and the selector's cause. If there is a medal for services to children's poetry, then John Foster should receive it. He has done so much through bright, colourful, cheerful, wide-ranging anthologies such as this to win poetry friends and influence poetry people.

Age range: 10–13+   TD

Themes: Animals, Circus, Night, School, Seasons

FOSTER, John (editor)

A Fourth Poetry Book

Oxford University Press, first published 1982, this 11th reprint 1994
126 pp, paperback, ISBN 0–19–918151–9, £3.50
Contents, Index of first lines, colour and b/w line illustrations, colour and b/w photographs

This collection maintains the high standard to be found throughout this excellent series. The fact that it is in its 11th printing since 1982 is a clear tribute to John Foster's skills as a selector. About a quarter of the 100 or so poems are making their first appearance in print: the rest are by no means tired, although there are some welcome favourites.

In one respect this particular volume is better than others in the series: there is a reliance on a smaller core of five artists. Their work is of high quality, marvellously complementary to the text. Moreover, it does not have that eye-wrenching clash of styles that is present in some of the other volumes. Free from any hint of text book tasks or teacherly guidance, the poems are there to be read and enjoyed in their own right.

Age range: 10–13+   TD

Themes: Animals, Family, Nature, School, Seasons

FOSTER, John (editor)

Another Fourth Poetry Book

Oxford University Press, first published 1989, this reprint 1993
127 pp, hardback ISBN 0–19–917126–2, paperback, ISBN 0–19–917125–4, £3.50
Contents, Index of first lines, colour and b/w line illustrations, colour and b/w photographs

The fact that there are fewer than 100 poems in this anthology reflects, perhaps, the older audience for whom these poems have been selected. It is reflected too in the more sombre expressions of some more serious, newly appearing themes – such as War. More of the poems are rather longer than in the 'lower' books in the series. Although there are some cruder illustrations to match the more obviously 'comic' poems, there seems to be a greater sensitivity and sobriety about much of the artwork (in which 10 artists have had a hand, often with remarkable distinction).

Like everything in this series, this book deserves a firm place in school and home libraries. There is material here for all.

Age range: 13–16+   TD

Themes: Family, Language, Natural World, The Sea, Sport, War

FOSTER, John (editor)
A Fifth Poetry Book
Oxford University Press, first published 1985, this reprint 1992
128 pp, hardback ISBN 0–19–916054–6, paperback, ISBN 0–19–916053–8, £3.50
Contents, Index of first lines, colour and b/w line illustrations, colour and b/w photographs

The six illustrators involved in this book (now its ninth printing) almost always hit the right, supportive note in a formula that has produced an eminently successful series. From *A Very First Poetry Book*, John Foster has sought to ensure a variety of poetic modes, tones, forms. Short poems, long poems, narrative poems, the reflective, the descriptive, the slight, the substantial, the strange, the familiar – are all here. The compiler leaves nothing much to chance in his attempts to win young and adolescent readers to the poetry cause.

Age range: 13–16+ TD

Themes: Age, Animals, Family, Nature, Seasons, Sport, War

FOSTER, John (editor)
Another Fifth Poetry Book
Oxford University Press, first published 1989, this reprint 1991
128 pp, hardback ISBN 0–19–917128–9, paperback, ISBN 0–19–917127–0
Contents, Index of first lines, colour and b/w line illustrations, colour and b/w photographs

The work of 14 artists and half-a-dozen photographs provide excellent support for this (seemingly) final anthology in John Foster's remarkable series. There are just over 90 poems in this particular collection, the usual recipe being adopted of providing a variety of moods, styles, structures, lengths, topics. The editor's aim of making poetry an inclusive art is demonstrated to perfection here; there is something to meet all tastes, something for the dipper-in, something for the long-distance poetry swimmer. A remarkable achievement.

Age range: 13–16+ TD

Themes: Environmental issues, Family, Landscape, Nature, Poetry, Seasons, Sport

FOSTER, John and PAUL, Korky (editors)
Dinosaur Poems
Oxford University Press, 1994
32 pp, paperback, ISBN 0–19–276126–9
Contents, Thematic, colour line illustrations

This anthology of dinosaur poems is wonderful to look at and appeals enormously to primary school children. John Foster offers us dinosaurs of all kinds in many situations and moods from 'At the Dinosaurs' Party' where 'They played HEAVY ROCK and then ROLLED in the slime' to 'Problem Solved' in which the mystery of the disappearance of the dinosaurs is finally solved. The poems are not easy but are made accessible by Korky Paul's brilliantly humorous illustrations.

Age range: 7–11 WEC

Theme: Dinosaurs

FOSTER, John (editor)
Dragon Poems
Oxford University Press, 1991, reprinted 1992
32 pp, paperback, ISBN 0–19–276108–0, £2.99
Contents, Thematic, colour line illustrations

There are 23 dragon poems here – illustrated in his usual robustly exuberant fashion by

Korky Paul. In keeping with the artwork, the bulk of the poems are humorous in content, with bouncy rhythms and tidy rhymes. The exceptions, in freer form and less frenetic in style, have their own kind of gentle attraction. Combining brisk wit and some pathos, *Dragon Poems* is likely to be seized on eagerly by young readers and to win friends for verse in general.

Age range: 10–14   TD

Theme: Dragons

FOSTER, John (compiler)

Dragon Poems

Oxford University Press, 1991, reprinted 1992 & 1993
16 pp, paperback, ISBN 0–19–916425–8, £1.50
Series: Oxford Poetry Paintbox, colour line illustrations

There are nine dragon poems here – illustrated unevenly by a range of (un-named) artists. Most are gently amusing and likely to appeal to confident young readers. Despite occasional uneasinesses in rhythm, the poems are generally tidily devised, offering in short space a fair range of tones. This is a slim collection likely to be reasonably well enjoyed by young readers.

Age range: 6–8+   TD

Theme: Dragons

FOSTER, John (compiler)

Dinosaur Poems/Emergency Poems/Home Poems/ Minibeast Poems/School Poems/Wizard Poems

Oxford University Press, 1994
each 16 pp, paperback, ISBN 0–19–916689–7, 0–19–916688–9, 0–19–916686–2,
0–19–916681–1, 0–19–916683–8, 0–19–916595–5
Series: Oxford Poetry Paintbox, Thematic, colour line illustrations

Poems for pre-school children, nursery and infant classes – many of them also in the longer Red, Yellow, Green and Blue Poetry Paintbox anthologies, also published in 1994 but offering a wide range of themes and a contents page and index. These theme-based, slim, 16-page books look at the themes above and the poetry is presented and illustrated in a lively and accessible way. These small books are useful to introduce the beginning reader to poetry but lack the browsability of the longer colour-named anthologies.

Age range: 4–7   WEC

Themes: Dinosaurs, Emergencies, Home, Magic, Minibeasts, School

FOSTER, John (compiler)

Egg Poems/Seed Poems/Sports Poems

Oxford University Press, 1991
each 16 pp, paperback, ISBN 0–19–916422–3, 0–19–916426–6, 0–19–916428–2
Thematic, colour line illustrations

Most of the poems in these books now appear in the Red, Yellow, Green and Blue Poetry Paintbox anthologies. Each of the 16-page books in this series contains around a dozen poems on a particular theme. They are child-friendly books aimed at the beginner reader and the poems do read aloud well. These three books are on rather less usual themes and contain poems that are simply fun as well as poems that will provoke further thought and discussion. The books are attractive and certainly don't make poetry seem daunting.

Age range: 4–7   WEC

Themes: Eggs, Seeds, Sport

FOSTER, John (compiler)

Transport Poems

Oxford University Press, 1994
16 pp, paperback, ISBN 0–19–916684–6, £1.50
Series: Oxford Poetry Paintbox, colour line illustrations

This volume follows the Poetry Paintbox series format – 8 poems, 7 illustrators, the contrasting styles of the latter diminishing the sense of coherence that might otherwise be attained. However, this is a better example of what the series has to offer. There is a greater air of conviction about the verse. There is more that children can identify with. The poetry cause will come to no harm if schools have this little book on a classroom or central library shelf.

Age range: 6–8+   TD
Theme: Transport

FOSTER, John (compiler)

Sea Poems

Oxford University Press, 1991, reprinted 1992
16 pp, paperback, ISBN 0–19–916424–X, £1.50
Series: Oxford Poetry Paintbox, Thematic, colour line illustrations

There are 11 poems here with, as in other books in the series, a variety of illustrators. It is not unfair, I think, to suggest that the signs of writing to meet market demands are less apparent here than in some of the other small anthologies. That is, there is a sense that the writers' hearts are firmly in the poems and less centred on the prospects of royalties. Most of the poems, though appropriately simple, do give signs of careful crafting. All are likely to receive positive responses from young readers.

Age range: 6–8+   TD
Theme: The Sea

FOSTER, John (editor)

Monkey Poems

Oxford University Press, 1993
16 pp, paperback, ISBN 0–19–916597–1
Series: Oxford Poetry Paintbox, Thematic, colour line illustrations

The Poetry Paintbox titles published by Oxford enjoy enormous popularity with beginner readers because the poems are short, easy to read and full of fun.

Each title in the series is 16 pages long and contains eight, nine or ten poems. Many of these are appearing in print for the first time, having been commissioned specifically by the editor, and a glance at the poets whose work is featured shows how well the editor is doing his job. Tony Bradman, Judith Nicholls, Julie Holder, Richard Edwards, Eric Finney, Brian Morse and Wes Magee are all contributors of note.

Though the quality of illustrations is a little unsteady these are bright, attractive, jaunty books which deserve a place in all nursery/infant libraries.

Age range: 3–6   JO

FOSTER, John (editor)

Space Poems

Oxford University Press, 1993
16 pp, paperback, ISBN 0–19–916596–3
Series: Oxford Poetry Paintbox, Thematic, colour line illustrations

A colourfully illustrated book of simple space poems. Most have a strong rhythmic quality that will appeal to the younger reader when reading aloud. Aliens and space races are a must. Two poems, however, offer more than the narrative style. 'Space Message' (Irene Rawnsley) nods in the direction of the care of the planet and 'From a Space Rocket' (Raymond Wilson) reflects about the beauty of space. A good 'dip into' class collection.

Age range: 5–7   MM
Theme: Space

FOSTER, John (editor)
Mouse Poems
Oxford University Press, 1993
16 pp, paperback, ISBN 0–19–916430–4
Series: Oxford Poetry Paintbox, Thematic, colour line illustrations

A short book (7 poems) of poems about mice, simple and direct for the younger reader, including a poetic version of the mouse and the lion fable. One poem in particular has a strong rhythm and repetition that will make access for a younger reader very easy ('The House's Tale' by Jean Kenward). The illustrations deserve a mention. They are all beautifully rich in colour and cover a range of styles.

Age range: 5–7   MM
Theme: Mice

FOSTER, John (editor)
Fox Poems
Oxford University Press, 1991
16 pp, paperback, ISBN 0–19–916423–1
Thematic, colour line illustrations

This is a small collection of seven poems about foxes. Four of these poems are narrative; in only one of these is the fox the victor – a poetic version of the fable *The Fox and Crow*. In other poems chickens and rabbits outfox the fox. They are good to read aloud, particularly 'The Corn Scratch, Kwa Kwa Hen and the Fox'. This has a strong rhythm which, together with imaginative language use, should encourage attentive listening –

> Grumbling, rumbling belly
> of the Slink Back Brush Tail Fox

The other poems explore the character and reality of the life of the fox; scavenging for food, exploring the town and providing for cubs.

Each illustrator captures the essence of the poem; they are very well chosen.

Age range: 6–9   MM
Themes: Animals, Fox

FOSTER, John (editor)
Giant Poems
Oxford University Press, 1993
16 pp, paperback, ISBN 0–19–916593–9
Series: Oxford Poetry Paintbox, Thematic, colour line illustrations

A varied collection of poems about giants; there are frightening giants, giant visitors and even a Fast Food Giant. An interesting inclusion is a narrative poem about an ogre. Two poems view giants from a different perspective; the human giants seen by ants ('Everything's giant', Charles Thomson) and an ant who is a giant when compared with a microbe ('All Giants', Eric Finney). Judith Nicholls, as usual, introduces imagery into 'Giant Tale'.

Illustrations are bright and colourful and all of them enhance the quality of the poems.

Age range: 5–8   MM

Theme: Giants

FOSTER, John (editor)

Twins Poems

Oxford University Press, 1993

16 pp, paperback, ISBN 0–19–916594–7

Series: Oxford Poetry Paintbox, Thematic, colour line illustrations

This is an interesting collection of poems about twins, all focusing on physical similarities and characteristics. Two poems, 'Which one are You?' (David Harmer) and 'Biff's Poem' (Roderick Hunt) do emphasise that twins, although similar, are different people. Two poems cheat a little for a collection about twins and use the ideas of mirror image and reflection and another, 'Twins' (Brian Moses), explores the closeness of friends that is almost twin-like.

The poems have simple language and clear messages. They are good to share – all rhyme and have a strong rhythm. There are lively illustrations by a range of illustrators.

Age range: 4–9   MM

Theme: Twins

FOSTER, John (editor)

Star Poems

Oxford University Press, 1993

16 pp, paperback, ISBN 0–19–916599–8

Series: Oxford Poetry Paintbox, Thematic, colour line illustrations

The collection of poems explores a range of stars; star fish, stars from Catherine Wheels, even a triangle star embedded in a poem describing how to draw a six-sided star (hexagram!).

The other poems focus more specifically on the night sky, including the Christmas star of Bethlehem.

The simple, pleasurable poems are ideal for reading aloud and sharing in groups.

Age range: 5–8   MM

Theme: Stars

FOSTER, John (editor)

Castle Poems

Oxford University Press, 1993

16 pp, paperback, ISBN 0–19–916598–X

Series: Oxford Poetry Paintbox, Thematic, colour line illustrations

A good collection of poems about castles. Two explore the history of the castle in terms of ghostly flashbacks and knights in armour. Others feature the traditional fairy tale where castles house princesses who need to be (and are) rescued. Building castles of blocks and sand bring castles to the present day and reality. The poems are strong enough to read aloud. The illustrations, from a variety of illustrators, capture the mood and content of each poem.

Age range: 4–8   MM

Theme: Castles

FOSTER, John (editor)

Water Poems

Oxford University Press, 1994
16 pp, paperback, ISBN 0–19–916680–3
Series: Oxford Poetry Paintbox, Thematic, colour line illustrations

Many aspects of water are contained in this brief collection of poems, rain, sea, swimming, washing.

Ian Souter's 'Great Water Giant' who pulls the plug in the sky, ends the poem visually with words arranged like rain-drops on the page. There is a simple, narrative poem, 'The day the hose flipped' (Eric Finney) which will amuse the younger readers.

The illustrations are very bright and appropriate. 'The Sea' by John Foster is given a semi-literal illustration of the sea like a bear and a cat.

The poems are, therefore, ideal to be shared, either with a large group or with a small number to talk about the poems and their illustrations and the layout of words on the page.

Age range: 6–11   MM
Theme: Water

FOSTER, John (chosen by)

A Red Poetry Paintbox/A Yellow Poetry Paintbox/
A Green Poetry Paintbox/A Blue Poetry Paintbox

Oxford University Press, 1994
64/64/96/96 pp, paperback, ISBN 0–19–916677–3, 0–19–916678–1, 0–19–916679–X
Series: Oxford Poetry Paintbox, Contents, Index, colour line illustrations

These four books are useful for introducing very young children to poetry and they all have a proper contents page and an index. The poems are full of rhyme and rhythm, or of what one five-year old called 'dancing words'. They are fun to read aloud and are complemented by colourful and varied illustrations. Children will quickly learn some of the rhymes and, once they can read, will love to read them to their friends.

The typeface, subject and level change with each book – Red being the easiest and Blue the hardest. *A Red Poetry Paintbox* (for children aged three and over) has large print and by the time readers have progressed to the *Blue* (for children aged six and over), the print is smaller and the presentation more sophisticated. The poems in the *Red* and the *Yellow* (for children aged four and over) books are about such things as colour, shape, cold things, big things, monsters, celebrations and pets, but by the *Green Poetry Paintbox* (for children aged five years and over), more serious issues such as birds being damaged by oil, recycling and litter are tackled through the poetry – but there's still a lot of fun as in 'Emergencies':

Red alert! Red alert! I've dropped my lolly in the dirt . . .

Age range: 3–6+   WEC

FOSTER, John (editor)

School's Out

Oxford University Press, 1988, reprints 1988–94
128 pp, paperback, ISBN 0–19–276078–5
Contents, Thematic, Index, b/w line illustrations

A perennially popular book of poetry (as the reprints testify). John Foster's collection of poems about school is a selection of light humorous verse dealing with teachers, school, dinners and playtime. Some of these have a seriousness underlying the humour ('School

Inspection', Raymond Wilson; a child's plea to think before answering). Interspersed with narrative and humour are poems that deal with more challenging and complex issues, such as the fear of the 'New Boy' (Nigel Cox) or of 'Swimming Lessons' (Gregory Harrison). They are accessible, however, for the younger reader and, because of the context, provide a subtle way of encouraging the reading of poems that make you think. Many of the poems capture the child's thinking (Ahlberg, as usual, a favourite). Anon also makes a contribution 'I love to do my homework' that surprises a laugh from the reader.

A good, light-hearted collection for an enjoyable read.

Age range: 8–14   MM

Theme: School

FOSTER, John (compiler)

Twinkle Twinkle Chocolate Box

Oxford University Press, 1991

102 pp, paperback, ISBN 0–19–276125–0

Contents, Index, colour line illustrations

A collection of rhymes for young children, some short and simple while others graduate to longer and more complex, for example the delightful nonsense of 'Alphabet of Horrible Habits' (Colin West) and a 'Caribbean Counting Rhyme' (Pamela Mordecai). Some have a lovely play on language 'escalator ate her' (John Walsh) or 'Dora Diller' (Jack Prelutsky), who has butterflies because she ate a caterpillar. A highly enjoyable book of rhymes to read, listen and to look at: the variety of bright and lively illustrations add to the delight.

Age range: 5–8   MM

Theme: Rhymes

FOSTER, John (editor)

New Angles, Book 1

Oxford University Press, 1987

115 pp, 2-book series, paperback, ISBN 0–19–833164–9

Contents, Indexes of titles and first lines, b/w line illustrations and photographs

John Foster is one of the most experienced and prolific editors whose work often includes specially commissioned pieces as well as previously unpublished poems. In appearance, style and quality *New Angles* has much the same feel as Geoffrey Summerfield's seminal series, *Voices*.

Here are poems, carefully juxtaposed to provide links and echoes and all of them speaking in a contemporary voice. And the range is impressive: John Agard on the strange English greeting, Howdooyoudoo; Valerie Bloom's challenging piece on patois; the hilarious newsreader in Tom Leonard's Unrelated Incident; Vernon Scannell reflecting on the word 'Death'; and James Berry asking what we do when faced with a difference.

This volume, and the second one in the series, *New Angles, Book 2*, are just the sort of thing to bring life and atmosphere to poetry work, and encourage the making of meanings in pupils of 12–16 years. Strongly recommended.

Age range: 12–16   JO

FOSTER, John (editor)
New Angles, Book 2
Oxford University Press, 1987
128 pp, 2-book series, paperback, ISBN 0–19–833165–7
Contents, Index, b/w line illustrations and photographs

John Foster became an anthologist because he was not very impressed with the poetry books available to him as a young teacher. He was wise to try his hand, and has made a significant contribution to the range of bright, attractive, engaging books now on the market.

Like *New Angles 1*, this is an impressive collection of lively, thought-provoking, amusing poems by writers like Rumens, Kit Wright, Scannell, Causley, Brownjohn, Pamela Gillilan and John Agard. The subjects are varied, as are the styles and moods, and the design layout adds to the sense of quality. Both books should be available to teachers working with lower secondary classes.

Age range: 12–16   JO

FOSTER, John (editor)
Spaceways
Oxford University Press, first published 1986, reprinted 1988, 1991, 1992
128 pp, hardback ISBN 0–19–276056–4, paperback ISBN 0–19–276068–8, £3.50
Contents, Thematics, Indexes of titles and first lines, b/w and colour line illustrations

Experienced anthologist, John Foster, has assembled here a most interesting collection of poems related in different ways to the theme of Space, roughly half of the 100 or so poems appearing in print for the first time. These poems range widely in style and mood from the trivially comic and absurd to the more reflective. They gain support too from five illustrators – although some may feel the clash of illustrative styles too hard to bear, as these range from brash cartoonery to subdued commentaries on the written word. One certainty about the anthology is that there is no pre-required interest in space matters – but that could well be developed by some of the verse encounters. More important, such is the variety of the verse that some space enthusiasts could be helped towards an appetite for poetry.

Age range: 11–16+   TD
Theme: Space

FOSTER, John (editor)
All in the Family
Oxford University Press, 1993
127 pp, paperback, ISBN 0–19–276119–6
Contents, Thematic, Index, b/w line illustrations

This is a well-balanced selection of poems about families. Humour and seriousness complement each other and allow the reader to explore depths of meaning and feeling as most of the poems have something definite to say about life and families. The problems and delights of adolescence are explored. Many are humorous but with an underlying sensitivity (e.g. 'Growing Pains' by Jean Little) and an exploration of the increasing complexity of emotions experienced when growing up.

Poems take everyday issues and problems, for example broken marriages ('What's your father' by James Kirkup) and children's guilt that often accompanies them ('Without Dad', Janet Greenyer) and their reactions ('Tug of War', John Kitching). The selection is always counter-balanced by positive views, in this case about re-marriage ('Stepmother', Jean Kenward). Different perspectives are offered on most topics.

The poems are useful for sharing and discussion. Some are ideal for reading aloud for fun ('Grandma can you rap?', Jack Ousbey).

The black and white illustrations that accompany the poems are sensitively drawn and add to the overall excellently presented book.

Age range: 9+   MM

Theme: Family

FOSTER, John and PAUL, Korky (editors)
Never Say Boo to a Ghost and other haunting rhymes
Oxford University Press, 1990
96 pp, paperback, ISBN 0–19–276089
Contents, Thematic, Index of first lines, of titles, b/w line illustrations

A good, ghoulish collection which will amuse children for most of the time. Vampires and werewolves are a popular amusement, together with ghosts that are frightened ('Tables Turned' by Michael Dugan). There is an unusual 'Small Ads' selection (Colin West's) for ghosts, monsters and witches.

Some of the poems have more than humour to commend them: the power of the imagination is explored ('Who's there?' by Ray Mather); nightmares are brought into the open ('Voice in the Night', by Joan Paulson). One or two, however, do leave a feeling of unease ('Locking Up' by Ian Serrailler) about ghostly powers.

The illustrations by Korky Paul fit the poems very well and are sufficiently cartoon-like to relieve the fear and let the reader sleep.

Age range: 9–14   MM

Themes: Ghosts, Vampires

FOSTER, John (editor)
Let's Celebrate: Festival Poems
Oxford University Press, 1989
111 pp, paperback, ISBN 0–19–276085–8
Contents, Thematic, Index of titles, of authors, of first lines, b/w and colour line illustrations, colour photographs

This is an extremely useful classroom book which can be used for poetry in its own right or poetry to complement the celebration of, or teaching about, celebrations and festivals from around the world. Many countries are represented in the poems although they are not all written by native speakers or celebrants.

There is a poem for every month and season and for the majority of festivals and different religious celebrations. Useful notes give a brief history or explanation as a background to the poems.

The majority of this collection is sincere and will encourage children to reflect upon the meaning that they have for themselves and for children in other cultures. Sensitively handled by teachers they may promote understanding and acceptance, particularly of others' religious ideologies.

The book is attractively presented with a combination of both black and white and colourful illustrations and a distinctive selection of photographs.

Age range: 5–12   MM

Themes: Celebration, Festivals, Religion

FULLER, Simon (editor)
The Poetry of Protest
BBC/Longman, first published 1991, reprinted 1993
128 pp, paperback, ISBN 0–563–34973–5, £4.75
Contents, Notes, b/w line illustrations and photographs

Most of the poems in this selection were included in a 1991 BBC Radio series with the book's present title. The introduction to the volume describes the intention to produce 'a varied and wide-ranging selection of poems especially suitable for study at GCSE or Standard Grade . . . There is a historical strand to the selection and a cross-cultural one'. Divided into five sections (Women's, Black, Workers', Prisoners' and Youth Voices), the book has also half-a-dozen pages of Notes and Reading/Response suggestions. Further support is given by carefully chosen black and white line and photographic illustrations. There is savagery here and bitterness – but there is also that remarkable weapon, humour. Sadly, the weakest section is that of the Youth Voices, admirable in sentiment, but suffering in comparison with the skilled expression of genuine grievance in the earlier sections. That said, the book will appeal strongly to the 15–16+ age group.

Age range: 15–16+   TD
Themes: Gender, Imprisonment, Protest, Race, Youth

FULLER, Simon (editor)
The Poetry of War
Longman, 1990
128 pp, paperback, ISBN 0–582–05811–2
Contents, Introduction, Reading and Responding to the poem, Useful Terms, war semantics

These poems were first broadcast by the BBC as part of a radio series for GCSE English. There are four sections to the book dealing with the two world wars, the nuclear problem, and war in our time. Each section is prefaced by a short, historical introduction and illustrated with black and white photographs.

The inclusion of a number of previously unpublished pieces, some by members of the Armed Services, others by civilian witnesses, adds to the power of this collection. The juxtaposition of poems by Scannell, Douglas, Zbigniew Herbert, Heaney and McGough with work by the new voices offers the reader a different perspective from most selections of war poetry. And, unusually, the suggested assignments recognise the need for the reader to ask questions and make meanings.

This is a successful compilation and is strongly recommended for use with the 15+ age group.

Age range: 15+   JO
Theme: War

H

HALLWORTH, Grace (remembered and collected by)
Buy a penny ginger and other rhymes
Longman, 1994
16 pp, paperback, ISBN 0–582–12101–9
Contents, colour illustrations

Grace Hallworth has chosen play rhymes from her childhood in Trinidad and Tobago as well as rhymes taught to her by children in this country. Some rhymes are familiar and some are new; one is offered in the original Swahili version as well as in English. There are instructions about the games to play or the actions to perform; they're in small print and quite complicated so very young children will need adult help the first time round but will quickly learn the rhymes. A good book for the nursery or infant classroom.

An audio cassette is also available.

Age range: 3–7   WEC

Theme: Play rhymes

HARRISON, Michael (collected by)

Splinters

Oxford University Press, 1988

120 pp, hardback, ISBN 0–19–276072–6, £4.95

Index of first lines, b/w illustrations

Splinters is a collection of some 110 or so very short poems – ranging from two to rarely more than four lines. They represent a range of moods from the light and trivial to the gently reflective to the quietly touching. Each 'Splinter' has a page to itself: most are quietly decorated by Sue Heap's neat, simple pen and ink illustrations. There are poems old, poems new, poems fresh, poems familiar, poems from near and far. A beautifully presented and sturdy little book, it has much to offer.

Age range: 11–16+   TD

Themes: Animals, Nature, Seasons

HARRISON, Michael and STUART-CLARK, Christopher (editors)

The Oxford Book of Christmas Poems

Oxford University Press, 1988

160 pp, paperback, ISBN 0–19–276080–7

Contents, Thematic, index, b/w and colour illustrations

This is an interesting, if rather serious collection of Christmas poems old and new, varied in form and length and illustrated by many artists in many styles. There are familiar pieces from poets such as Ted Hughes, John Betjeman, T.S. Eliot and Charles Causley as well as a few humorous touches from young poets like Mick Gowar, short pithy poems from U.A. Fanthorpe, images of Christmas in Australia, Africa and Mexico, and there's 'Christmas Day in the Workhouse' dramatically illustrated by Charles Keeping. A wide-ranging collection in which there is sure to be something that connects with every view of Christmas.

Age range: 11+   WEC

Theme: Christmas

HARRISON, Michael and STUART-CLARK, Christopher (editors)

The Oxford Book of Animal Poems

Oxford University Press, 1992

157 pp, hardback, ISBN 0–19–276105–6

Contents, Thematic, Index of animals, authors, artists, titles, first lines, b/w and colour line illustrations

This must be one of the most beautiful poetry books recently published. The poems are about birds, animals and insects from all over the world, ranging from elephant to flea! Many of the poems are translated for the book. They all reveal the beauty, strength and habitats of the animals and only a few of the poems focus on the humorous aspect of the animal; the majority are thoughtful and sensitive and provide a challenge for the reader.

The illustrations, by a range of illustrators, capture moods, colour and movement and often manage to combine two or more poems.

A book worthy of any collection, whether classroom or personal.

Age range: 8–18+   MM

Themes: Animals, Birds, Insects

HARRISON, Michael and STUART-CLARK, Christopher (editors)
A Year Full of Poems
Oxford University Press, 1991

144 pp, hardback, ISBN 0–19–276097–1

Contents, Thematic, Index, b/w and colour illustrations

A very special anthology for classroom or library. The poems are full of variety and demonstrate many different ways of writing poetry. The look of the book is good; it is a book you will want to hold and browse through, and the illustrations, by lots of artists and in many different styles, work well to establish mood and to complement the words. There are splashes of full colour, line drawings, woodcuts and misty, moody pictures in shades of grey and black and they all serve to focus on the poetry not to take over from it.

The poems really do offer the moods of the year; it's so comforting to discover that someone else is pleased 'that February is something purely temporary'. The poems are old and new, full of atmosphere and opinion, humour and seriousness, imagery and story and the poets are the greats of the past and the present alongside some new names.

A challenging book made very accessible by good design; it deserves many careful readings.

Age range: 8–18   WEC

Themes: Months, Seasons

HARRISON, Michael and STUART-CLARK, Christopher (editors)
Narrative Poems
Oxford University Press, 1981, reprints 1990, 1992

188 pp, paperback, ISBN 0–19–831245–8

Contents, Index of titles, of authors, a few b/w illustrations

There are 55 narrative poems in this collection. At least a third of them are pretty familiar, with names such as Tennyson, Southey, Longfellow and that old favourite Anon in the Index of Authors. The living, however, also have a firm place in that list – as do writers from Canada, Australia and elsewhere. There are only a few illustrations, but they are generally of impressive quality in what otherwise is a book whose appearance is somewhat utilitarian. That said, there are many poems, for instance by Stevie Smith, by Charles Causley, by Vernon Scannell and a number of the newer and older ballads that, well-presented, are capable of appealing to youngsters in the middle years of secondary schooling.

Age range: 13–16+   TD

Themes: Adventure, Death, Ghosts, Mystery, Romance

HARRISON, Michael and STUART-CLARK, Christopher (editors)
The Oxford Book of Story Poems
Oxford University Press, 1990, reprinted 1991

176 pp, hardback, ISBN 0–19–276087–4,, £9.95

Contents, Thematic, Index of first lines, of titles, of authors, of artists, colour illustrations

There are some 66 narrative poems in this sturdy book. They cover various themes in a variety of fashions and moods. They have the benefit of high quality colour illustrations by a dozen or so excellent artists. The classic narrative poems are here – 'Listener', 'Jabberwocky', 'La Belle Dame', 'Inchcape Rock', 'Pied Piper', 'Highwayman' – and so on. They are complemented by more recent story poems, by poets such as Charles Causley, Mick Gowar, Michael Rosen, *et al*. Variation of length, style, mood, structure is in plain evidence in a collection that is eminently useful and designed well to give proper pleasure.

Age range: 9–13+   TD

Themes: Animals, Journeys, Monsters, Mystery, Nonsense, People, The Sea

HARRISON, Michael and STUART-CLARK, Christopher (editors)
The Oxford Treasury of Children's Poems
Oxford University Press, 1988
176 pp, paperback, ISBN 0–19–276134–X
Contents, Index, b/w and colour illustrations

A wide-ranging collection of poetry by poets both traditional and modern and covering many moods and subjects. This is a good book for dipping into and for browsing as there are so many eye-catching pages. The use of many illustrators takes away the sense of wholeness and offers instead such variety that there is sure to be something for every child to enjoy, but there are times when the words are so much better than the illustrations. A good collection of poetry to give children hours of enjoyment, poetry that they will love to read to each other.

Age range: 4–10   WEC

HARRISON, Michael and STUART-CLARK, Christopher (editors)
Young Dragon Book of Verse
Oxford University Press, 1989
168 pp, paperback, ISBN 0–19–831259–8
Contents, Thematic, Index, b/w line illustrations

A good variety of poems, old and new, carefully chosen for quality of content. There are a number of themes separated by carefully drawn illustrations; individual poems are also interspersed with illustrations.

The themes inevitably include School ('Door of the Classroom') with the almost inevitable negative attitudes to and remembrances of school. This is unfortunate – poems that express the positive side of teaching and learning would be an asset in poetry books used in school. One poem, 'Crystals' (Barrie Wade) does focus on the wonder of learning.

There are suggestions at the end of the book for readers (teachers?) which are designed to facilitate discussion and writing. Some are, unfortunately, a bit 'teacher-led' – for example, 'Explain the title of this poem'. There is the danger that such suggestions discourage, rather than encourage, the joy of reading poetry.

Age range: 8–14   MM

Themes: Animals, Classroom, Dreams, Fantasy, Weather

HARRISON, Michael and STUART-CLARK, Christopher (editors)
The New Dragon Book of Verse
Oxford University Press, 1977, this reprint 1994
264 pp, paperback ISBN 0–19–831241–5, hardback ISBN 0–19–831240–7
Contents, Thematic as found in opening contents, Index of titles/first lines, of authors,
Postscript by Sir John Betjeman, b/w illustrations

With 18 printings between 1977 and 1988, this anthology was revised and enlarged in

1989 and has been reprinted four times since. This record is remarkable testimony to the deservedly high regard in which the book is held. Its emphasis is declaredly on English poetry. So, while there are poems from the entire British Isles and some American interlopers, there are no signs of new voices from much further afield. That said, with the bulk of the poems from familiar, older, more established sources, there are important contributions from more recent times by such poets as Patricia Beer, Charles Causley, Ted Hughes, Edwin Brock, Seamus Heaney, *et. al.* The fact that poems by male poets outnumber those by female poets by about 20 to 1 could raise some interested eyebrows, of course!

Age range: 12–16+   TD

Themes: Childhood, Creatures, Landscape, Mystery, People, Reflection, Seascapes, War

HARRISON, Michael and STUART-CLARK, Christopher (editors)
Poems 1

Oxford University Press, 1979

96 pp, (ISBN 0–19–834267–5), paperback, ISBN 0–19–834267–5

Series: Books 1 & 2, plus Teacher's edition, Contents, Index, b/w line illustrations and photographs

The editors have set out to interest 10–14-year-olds by collecting a wide range of poems which they have put together in two volumes. The first of these, *Poems 1*, covers the first two years in the secondary school.

The strength of these books lies in the vitality of the chosen poems. There is a rough, noisy, knockabout, amusing feel to many of them, with playground rhymes, jokes, shape poems and riddles rubbing shoulders with ballads, lyrics and more formal pieces. In *Poems 2*, the editors introduce themes which will appeal to 12–14-year-olds, without sacrificing in any way the narrative vigour and interest of the first book.

Used in conjunction with the companion volume, *Writing Poems*, these are attractive, useful books for children to use directly and teachers to have available as source material. They are extremely well illustrated with eye-catching black and white photographs and graphics. All three are strongly recommended.

Age range: 10–13   JO

HARRISON, Michael and STUART-CLARK, Christopher (editors)
Poems 2

Oxford University Press, 1980

125 pp, (ISBN 0–19–834269–1), paperback, ISBN 0–19–834268–3

Series: Poems 1 & 2, plus Teacher's edition, Contents, Cassette 0–19–840315–1, b/w line illustrations and photographs

See *Poems 1* above.

Age range: 13–14   JO

HARRISON, Michael and STUART-CLARK, Christopher (editors)
Bright Star Shining – Poems for Christmas

Oxford University Press, 1993

48 pp, hardback, ISBN 0–19–279926–6

Contents, Thematic, Index of titles, of authors, of first lines, colour line illustrations

This anthology of Christmas poems is ideal for younger readers. It is a mixture of poems about the celebration of the Christmas season and of the events surrounding the nativity. The latter are viewed from different perspectives; animals, the inn-keeper's wife, the shepherds and Mary. The poems do capture some of the sense of wonder that children can share. One final poem (so final it appears after the index and acknowledgements) ends the book on a slightly irreverent but humorous note – one suspects it is for the adults, rather than children who read the book.

The illustrations by Stephen Lambert, Louise Rawlings and Susan Scott vary in style but enhance the simplicity of the poems.

Age range: 5–8   MM
Theme: Christmas

HARRISON, Michael and STUART-CLARK, Christopher (editors)
Peace and War
Oxford University Press, 1989
208 pp, paperback, ISBN 0–19–276071–8
Contents, Index of titles, of first lines, b/w line illustrations

A book that inevitably, perhaps, has many more poems about War than Peace. Peace, however, starts the collection; the peace of family, night and countryside – although even in the last category, images of war creep into images of the countryside, culminating in war against nature itself ('Rural Idyll' by Margaret Tems).

The collection embraces poems from Ancient Greece and Rome, from the Bible and through to the atomic bomb and Vietnam ('What were they like?', Denise Levertov). The poems are from many different countries; Russia, Korea, Australia, China, Hungary, Poland, Zululand, America and England.

Inevitably the War poems focus on the futility and loss (collectively and individually) of war for victor and vanquished. Very few refer to glory and honour – more to the longing for peace ('Lessons of the War: II Judging Distances' by Henry Reed).

The book begins and ends with peace but the longing for peace appears as the central theme.

A powerful and emotive collection; reflective and penetrating. It would be wonderful to use for discussion in the classroom, not only about poetic form, but about response and attitude. The illustrations by Alan Marks, although understated and few, capture moments of peace and war, even when depicting a phone, a hand and a fat cigar!

Age range: 12–16+   MM
Themes: Peace, War

HEANEY, Seamus
New Selected Poems, 1966–1987
Faber and Faber, 1990
250 pp, paperback, ISBN 0–571–14372–5, £6.99
Contents, Index

None of the work in this volume is directed at children, but there is no doubt that the selections from 'Death of a Naturalist', 'Door into the Dark' and 'Wintering Out' especially can speak with particular power to thoughtful adolescents, leading them on to some of the more demandingly obscure (or less seemingly transparent) later work. The cover's reference to Seamus Heaney's 'prodigious talent' is undeniably correct. The more young readers who can encounter it, the better for them and for the world they inhabit. Few other contemporary poets can offer them, to the same degree, Seamus Heaney's remarkable blend of skill, direct observation and sensitive insight.

Age range: 14–16+   TD
Themes: Childhood, Ireland, Nature, Rural life

HEANEY, Seamus and HUGHES, Ted (editors)

The Rattle Bag

Faber and Faber, 1982
475 pp, paperback, ISBN 0–571–11976–X
Contents, Index, Glossary

Published in 1982, this lengthy volume still sets the standard for poetry anthologies, and the chosen verse sings and rocks and shakes like the *Rattle Bag* from which it takes its name. Heaney and Hughes have picked poems from a wide range of sources – tribal cultures, chants and charms, epitaphs, ballads and songs – and set them alongside some of the best poetry ever written.

The editors' decision to arrange the poems alphabetically by title, is a further bonus, offering each reader a chance to dip into the 'bag' to discover the delights it contains. Thus Emily Dickinson is found next to Walter Raleigh; Ginsberg follows Eliot; and Hyam Plutzik sits well between Blake and Burns.

The Rattle Bag is a marvellous resource for children and teachers. It caters for all tastes and all ages, and should be in regular use in both primary and secondary schools.

Age range: 7–16+   JO
Themes: Songs, Spells and charms

HEATH, R.B. (editor)

Trade Winds

Longman, 1990, third impression 1993
190 pp, paperback, ISBN 0–582–02195–2
Contents, Thematic, Glossary, Biographical detail section, b/w and colour photographs

There are almost 100 poems here from Chinese, Indian, Pakistani, African and Caribbean cultures, cross-referenced by such themes as: Love, Nature, Death, War, Poverty, Women, Work, etc. Alongside these often demanding riches, there is earnest pedagogical intent – aimed at the student (e.g. 'What are the main differences between the transliteration and the versification?'). After each poem has made its appearance there are 'discussion points' of a pretty traditional kind – 'What is the setting for the poem?' 'Is there a reason for the shape of the poem?' – plus some unnerving Written Work suggestions. ('Write your own harvest festival poem.' 'Write a paragraph or two explaining what you feel'.)

At the end of the book there are further oral and written coursework suggestions – the former a little more innovative than the latter.

This is another of those anthologies whose success in adventurously drawing together interesting and generally unusual material has to be set alongside the somewhat heavy-handed pedagogical purpose. The danger is that the classroom strength of the material could be sapped by that teaching design.

However, the material here ought to command attention: the book could have a useful place on the English Department's Staff library shelf. It could give support to less than confident teachers.

Age range: 14–16+   TD
Themes: Childhood, Countryside, Famine, Freedom, Love, Nature, Peace, Poverty, Slavery, War, Work

HULSE, Michael; KENNEDY, David; MORLEY, David (editors)

The New Poetry

Bloodaxe, 1993, this third impression 1994
350 pp, paperback, ISBN 1–85224–244–2
Series: Bloodaxe Books (Poetry Format), Contents, Biographical Notes

Described on the cover as 'The first anthology of the new British and Irish poets of the 80s and 90s', this 350-page blockbuster comprises some 233 poems by 55 writers. The cover quotes Alan Brownjohn's *Sunday Times* review – 'A generation of poets full of verse and promise – and achievement'. It also refers to Sean O'Brien's view that the anthology 'reveals a vigorous art, formally intelligent and unabashedly political'. As with '60 Women Poets', however, from the same publishers, it is difficult to see this as a 'poetry book for children'. The concerns here and the language in which they are expressed put the book firmly in the adult world. It is difficult to escape the belief that only the rarest of 6th Formers would borrow it from the school library – despite the presence of poets such as Liz Lochhead, Linton Kwesi Johnson, Ian McMillan and Simon Armitage.

Age range: 16+   TD

Theme: Britain in decline, Politics, Science, Urban Scene, The

J

JACKSON, David (selected by)

The Way to the Zoo

Oxford University Press, 1983 (hbk) (First pbk 1989), this reprint 1990
128 pp, paperback, ISBN 0–19–276079–3, £3.95
Contents, Index of first lines, of titles, b/w illustrations

This is a useful anthology, although it is superficially less appealing than some others in the same field because of the lack of colour in the illustrations, fine though the work of the three artists involved may be. Mixing the fresh with the familiar, David Jackson's anthology takes an important step forward, however, in seeking to introduce young readers to work from Australia, the Indian sub-continent, from Africa, from North America and elsewhere – in addition to well-chosen material by children as poets. There is flexibility of form; there is flexibility of tone; there is the happily slight alongside the weightier. A pleasant and useful book with big, bold print.

Age range: 7–12+   TD

Theme: Animals

K

KING, Karen (compiler)
Illustrated by BECK, Ian

Oranges and Lemons

Oxford University Press, 1985
48 pp, paperback, ISBN 0–19–27228–6
Contents, colour illustrations

This book presents traditional and modern singing and dancing games: it gives the words, the music and illustrated instructions on how to play. The layout is clear and attractive – one rhyme to each double-page spread, with instructions and music on the left and words and illustration on the right. This is a great book for sharing; the games work well with quite large groups of children.

Ian Beck's style is very appealing – there's one wordless double-page spread that puts together the animals who pop in and out of the book in an exciting party scene that is lots of fun to talk about.

A cassette is available to accompany this book.

Age range: 2–6   WEC

Theme: Dancing, Games, Singing

L

LANGLEY, Jonathan (illustrator)

(a) ## The Collins Book of Nursery Rhymes
HarperCollins, 1990
96 pp, hardback, ISBN 0–00–183163–1
Contents, Index, colour illustrations

(b) ## Nursery Rhymes – Book One
HarperCollins, 1992
32 pp, paperback, ISBN 0–00–664132–6
Contents, Index, colour illustrations

(c) ## Nursery Rhymes – Book Two
HarperCollins, 1992
32 pp, paperback, ISBN 0–00–664133–4
Contents, Index, colour illustrations

The Collins Book of Nursery Rhymes is a wonderful gift book. The rhymes are cleverly arranged under a theme for each double-page spread. For example, under the heading, 'What's for Dinner?', there are six rhymes – 'Polly put the Kettle on', 'Davy Davy Dumpling', 'Little Tommy Tucker', 'Little Miss Muffet', 'Pease Porridge Hot' and 'Jack Sprat'. There's a lot of fun in this book, particularly in such sections as 'Bad Boys and Naughty Girls'.

Jonathan Langley's illustrations are very child-centred and really appeal to the very young. This is a good first nursery rhyme book for home and school.

HarperCollins have selected titles from this book and published them, with the same illustrations, in two shorter books in the Picture Lions series under the titles, *Nursery Rhymes Book One* and *Book Two*. These paperbacks look beautiful and are even more user-friendly than the full collection.

Age range: 2+   WEC

General theme: Nursery rhymes

LEWIS, Naomi (editor)

Messages
Faber and Faber, 1985
255 pp, paperback, ISBN 0–571–13647–8
Contents, Thematic, Index of authors, of first lines, Short (3 pp) introduction

In 1985 Naomi Lewis put together an outstanding collection of poems in her anthology, *Messages*. She included a number of well-known poems on the grounds that they would be new to many readers; she selected poems which could, with profit, be re-visited; she chose not-so-familiar works which appealed to her, and she found a number of new poems never before seen in anthologies.

There are more than 180 poems in the book, divided into 9 sections roughly according to subject. They provide an excellent introduction, for secondary children, to poetry which is mainly from this century. They will surely help to stimulate discussion and investigation into the nature and function of poetry in today's society.

This collection is a 'must' for all English departments, and one which all English specialists will expect to use.

Age range: 11–16　　　　　　　　　　　　　　　　　　　　　　　　　　JO

Themes: Childhood, Dreams, Family, Relationships, Stories, The Wild

LINES, Kathleen (compiler)
Lavender's Blue

Oxford University Press, 1954, this reprint 1992
180 pp, paperback, ISBN 0–19–272208–5, £5.95
Index of first lines, b/w and colour illustrations

Although Harold Jones' black and white and colour illustrations have now a somewhat faded and subdued air, this collection of nursery rhymes, first published in 1954 and reprinted since over 20 times, continues to house a most comprehensive store of this particular tradition. Time may perhaps have eroded the strength of praise accorded by earlier critics but there is still much of genuine value here. Indeed, the shifts in illustrative style could offer food for thought in their own right.

Age range: 0–5+　　　　　　　　　　　　　　　　　　　　　　　　　　TD

Theme: Nursery rhymes

LIVINGSTON, Myra Cohn (editor)
Cat Poems

Oxford University Press, 1994
32 pp, paperback, ISBN 0–19–276131–5
Contents, Thematic, b/w illustrations

A collection of cat poems to delight cat lovers, illustrated with subtle, life-like cats in shaded black and white. There are cats of all kinds, in all moods, they're sleeping, hunting, playing, turning into princesses and sleeping again. There are old favourites like Eleanor Farjeon's 'Cat' – that 'sleeky flatterer, spitfire chatterer' and Eliot's 'The Song of the Jellicles' as well as some less well-known ones. The end result is a real celebration of cats.

Age range: 5–12　　　　　　　　　　　　　　　　　　　　　　　　　　WEC

Theme: Cats

LIVINGSTON, Myra Cohn (editor)
Dog Poems

Oxford University Press, 1994
30 pp, paperback, ISBN 0–19–276139–0
Contents, Thematic, b/w line illustrations

A small collection of poems about dogs which encompasses puppies to old dogs, birth to death. Inevitably, perhaps, in a book that has its focus upon pets there are many poems which are sentimental in approach – although it is unlikely that dog lovers will find that a disadvantage. They do explore, however, the relationships between dogs and their owners – the love and affection that one inspires in the other. 'Stories', by J. Patrick Lewis, reminds the reader, unsentimentally of the differences in life span between the two, something that is particularly hard for children to come to terms with.

The illustrations by Leslie Morrill capture the mood of the poems beautifully. The very safe line drawings complement the nostalgic/sentimental aspect of the poems, but one illustration for 'Dog' by William Jay Smith, is great fun as dogs are 'dressed' in (in)appropriate clothes!

Age range: 8–14   MM

Theme: Animals, Dogs

M

McCLURE, Gillian (editor)
Poems that Go Bump in the Night
Simon and Schuster, 1994
30 pp, paperback, ISBN 0–7500–1431–8, £3.99
Contents, coloured illustrations

Two dozen 'creepy' poems are energetically and colourfully illustrated here by the selector. She offers touches of the comic amongst the more or less disturbing. Favourite names predominate, a small clutch of Traditionalists and Anons joined by such familiars as Milligan, Monro, Causley, de la Mare, McGough. For those who are 'into' ghosts, witches and the weird, this is an attractive and not inordinately expensive collection.

Age range: 9–12   TD

Themes: Ghosts, Witches

McKEE, David (illustrator)
Our Favourite Rhymes
Longman, 1964
32 pp, paperback, ISBN 0–582–12087–X
Series: The Book Project, Contents, coloured illustrations

Thirteen well-known nursery rhymes, illustrated with great style and imagination by David McKee. His mini-pictures on the endpapers offer lots to talk about as do all the rather unusual illustrations. A very user-friendly first nursery rhyme book. It is good to see books published as part of a reading scheme looking so good.

One of the 'Read Aloud' books in Longman's The Book Project.

Age range: 3–6   WEC

Theme: Nursery Rhymes

McMULLEN, Eunice (compiler)
One of Your Legs is Both The Same
Pan Macmillan, 1994
104 pp, hardback, ISBN 0–333–60471–7, £7.99
Contents, Index of authors and first lines (joint), b/w illustrations

Illustrated by Colin McNaughton with his usual bold extravagance, this is a collection of 51 poems by Adrian Henri, Terry Jones, Michael Rosen, Kit Wright – and CM himself. About 80% of the poems have appeared before, some having their origins well over ten years ago. Nonetheless, they make an appealingly welcome reappearance here. It's almost entirely a 'nonsense' collection – with interesting differences detectable in the work of each of the poets. Talk about those differences could pay remarkable and pleasurable language-awareness dividends with young readers. They will also take some pleasure in the poets' autobiographical sketches at the end of a slim volume which is likely to prove popular with older primary and younger secondary pupils.

Age range: 8–11+   TD

Themes: Animals, Animal Rights, Ghosts, Humour, Nonsense, School

MITCHELL, Adrian (editor)

Strawberry Drums

Simon and Schuster, 1990
39 pp, paperback, ISBN 0–7500–0364–2
Contents, Coloured line illustrations

This is a collection of poems chosen by Adrian Mitchell primarily for their strong rhythmic quality and because he likes them! Traditional rhythms are included (for example, 'Lullaby' – a song of the Eskimo people of Greenland) as are the more traditional poets (for example, Blake's 'The Tyger' and de la Mare's 'Silver').

They are all poems to be read aloud or, as Adrian Mitchell suggests, to dance to or to be turned into songs and paintings. Most importantly, they are to be enjoyed.

There is even a 'do-it-yourself' section with helpful hints for writing poetry using poems by Michael Rosen and Adrian Mitchell as models.

The illustrations by Frances Lloyd are light and refreshing.

A good collection for the classroom.

Age range: 7–11   MM

N

NICHOLLS, Judith (editor)

Earthways – Poems on Conservation

Oxford University Press, 1993
96 pp, paperback, ISBN 0–19–272248–4
Contents, Thematic, Index, b/w and coloured illustrations

This is a very special anthology; the selection is made by Judith Nicholls with her usual sure touch. The theme is conservation; the poems look at the destruction of the environment and the loss of animals and move on to a more positive mood, encouraging the reader to 'enjoy the earth gently'. There is splendid language in these poems which are very varied in form and content. The design of the book is exceptional – good cover and layout, good use of space, typography and colour – and the result is a book children will want to pick up, read and talk about.

Age range: 8–16   WEC
Theme: Conservation

NICHOLLS, Judith (editor)

What On Earth . . .?

Faber and Faber, 1989
118 pp, paperback, ISBN 0–571–15262–7
Contents, Thematic, Index, b/w illustrations

Judith Nicholls is a very sure anthologiser and has put together here poems about the beauty of the world and of conservation that will stimulate thought and help young readers realise the power of poetry. There are anonymous poems from other cultures, poems from classic poets such as John Clare, Gerard Manley Hopkins and Wordsworth and contributions from many contemporary poets. I couldn't be without this anthology in a secondary school classroom.

Age range: 10+   WEC
Theme: Conservation

NICHOLLS, Judith (editor)
Wordspells
Faber and Faber, 1988
132 pp, paperback, ISBN 0–571–16909–0
Contents, Index, b/w illustrations

Judith Nicholls writes in her introduction: 'The best poetry sings and illuminates . . . The best poems are those which help us to look, and to see and feel more clearly than we might otherwise have done' and she really offers such poems. The subject of the anthology is really the magic of words and the reader feels that magic in riddles, poems by children, by contemporary poets and by the great poets of the past. A most inviting book for readers in the lower secondary school.

Age range: 9+   WEC

O

OPIE, Iona and Peter (editors)
I Saw Esau
Walker Books, 1947
160 pp, hardback, ISBN 0–7445–2151–3
Contents, Introductory notes, colour line illustrations

There is a fascinating account in Iona Opie's introduction to this book, of the changes which came about when it was decided to update the original collection. Some rhymes were taken out and others put in, but the most radical change arose when Maurice Sendak agreed to provide illustrations for this delightful compilation. The result is a book to relish and treasure.

The fact is that the riddles, repartee, insults, graces, incantations and lullabies are greatly strengthened by Sendak's incomparable pictures. Soggy babies and monstrous creatures; cubs, kings and beggarmen; ducks that drive lorries, and cats in hats with torn skin, provide additional boisterous and colourful entertainment. Even the notes are punctuated with appropriate illustrations.

This edition, published in 1992, would make a splendid present for a special child, and should, in any case, be part of the book provision in all nursery and infant libraries. The only slight doubt about the book is that it is sub-titled 'a school child's pocket book'. The dimensions are in keeping with that description, but not the weight! Schools that are unable to afford a copy should buy two, on approval, and raffle one to pay for the other.

Age range: 3–16+   JO

OPIE, Iona and Peter (editors)
The Oxford Nursery Rhyme Book
Oxford University Press, 1955
224 pp, hardback, ISBN 0–19–869112–2
Contents, Thematic, Index, Preface, Sources of illustrations, b/w line illustrations

'Gathered here are 800 rhymes and ditties. They are the infant riddles, jingles, catches, tongue-trippers, baby games, toe-names, maxims, alphabets, counting rhymes, prayers and lullabies, with which generation after generation of mothers and nurses have attempted to please the youngest.' So said the Opies in 1955 when this collection was first published, and this is a perfect description of the book's contents.

The instructive preface points out that de la Mare once remarked that rhymes such as these 'free the fancy, charm tongue and ear, delight the inward eye' and can lead the way to poetry itself.

There are 600 illustrations – many of them woodcuts that accompanied the rhymes when they first appeared in toybooks – plus 150 specially commissioned designs by Joan Hassall. Put all these together and you have a book which will charm adults as well as children, and is simply the best of its kind.

Age range: 0–5   JO
Themes: Ballads, Lullabies, People, Riddles, Songs, Wonders

OPIE, Iona and Peter (editors)
The Oxford Book of Children's Verse
Oxford University Press, 1973
407 pp, hardback, ISBN 0–19–812140–7
Contents, Indexes by author, first line and familiar title, Notes on authors and sources

A collection of children's poems chronologically arranged by date of publication from medieval (Chaucer) to the present century (for example, Kipling, A.A. Milne and T.S. Eliot).

There is an extensive range of topics, poets and types of poems. Children will enjoy listening to many of the earlier poems and listening to and reading some of the later ones, for example Lear, Nash and Eliot.

For the adult reader there is a useful introduction which gives interesting historical information and notes about authors and sources at the end.

The anthology is possibly of more interest to the adult, rather than the child reader. Nevertheless it deserves a place in all classrooms as all the poems are of interest.

Age range: 2–16+   MM

ORME, David (editor)
Cheating at Conkers
Longman, 1994
47 pp, paperback, ISBN 0–582–12201–5
Series: The Book Project, Contents, Thematic, b/w line illustrations

'How to Cheat at Conkers and Win' (David Harmer) is typical of the many humorous and irreverent poems that make up this collection. There are poems about school, going home from school and home itself, plus a section on dreams and fantasies. The latter includes 'The Tale of the Leprechauny Man and the Unsuccessful Fishery Expedishery' (Gerard Benson) which cleverly plays with words, for example, 'tripping carelessly over a mounting pique' which may be too sophisticated for some children to appeciate fully. Sue Cowling's poem 'Christmas Stocking' also uses word play, but with words that have not yet appeared in the English dictionary; this will surely encourage children to use their own word inventions when words they know just will not do!

None of the poems is taxing but Dave Calder's 'Greengrocer' and Alexis Lykiard's 'Garden Enthusiasts' may encourage children to reflect more deeply on what they have read. The bold and dramatic illustrations by Derek Collins complement the poems most successfully.

Age range: 7–11   MM
Themes: Dreams, Home, School

ORME, David and GLYNN, Martin (editors)
Doin Mi Ed in: Rap Poems
Piper 1993
64 pp, paperback, ISBN 0–330–32817–4, £2.99
Contents, Introduction: How to write and perform rap

David Orme and Martin Glynn have collected 27 rap poems, many of them new to this reviewer. There is a short introduction which explains the meaning of rap and dub, and indicates where they started and how they grew, and then the editors advise young readers on how to perform rap.

Here you will find an Ozone rap, a Yucky rap, a Baby rap and a Tell-tale rap; a Bored rap, a Ghost Town rap, a Disco rap and a Rice pudding rap; there is even a Gujerati rap. By the time you get to the 27th rap you may feel like this:

> I've had enough of rappin' –
> Know what I mean?
> I've lost my voice rappin'
> On the happy rappin' scene.
> I've lost my voice rappin', I've lost my voice;
> I've lost my voice rappin' – ain't got no choice –
> I'm wrappin' up the raps 'cos I've lost my voice.

Great fun, and at £2.99 a good buy. Organise a Rap contest; publish your own rap poems; use this as a guide.

Age range: 9–14   JO
Theme: Rap

ORME, David and SALE, James (editors)
Poetry Street 1, 2 and 3
Longman, 1991
90 pp, paperback, ISBN 0–582–03924–X
Series: Poetry Street, Contents, Partial thematic, b/w and colour line illustrations

What a splendid idea of the editors to invite a well known poet to contribute to each of the books in this series – and even better when the writers turn out to be Judith Nicholls in Book 1, James Berry in Book 2, and Wendy Cope in the final volume.

Each book begins with simple advice, emphasising the right of the pupil to read and enjoy before embarking on other activities, and each book contains three major sections – About Us; About Poets; About Poems. The editors have succeeded in selecting poems which will amuse, challenge, disturb and provoke young readers, and sections One and Three are used to stimulate positive responses from pupils.

There is a good mixture of old and new poems, of familiar and unfamiliar pieces. In the middle section the guest poet makes a personal contribution, using his/her own poems and selecting ones they like written by other poets, and offers advice about developing and constructing poems. Three excellent books, each of which will add considerably to a classroom library.

Age range: 10–13   JO
Theme: People, Poets

P

PARK, Julie (editor)
Giggly Rhymes
Little Mammoth, 1989
30 pp (unnumbered), paperback, ISBN 0–7497–0217–6
Colour illustrations

The book is a selection of poems chosen by the illustrator and it's the illustrations that are the selling point. There is so much to look at that the poems are almost secondary. The illustrations are a delight; they are colourful, witty; they extend and enhance the familiar rhymes. They contain visual jokes and verbal comment. Every page is lively and stimulating.

Poems are OK too – all familiar, tried and tested.
Age range: 4–16+   MM

PARK, Julie (editor)
More Giggly Rhymes
Little Mammoth, 1991
30 pp, paperback, ISBN 0–7497–0311–3
Coloured line illustrations

A collection of nineteen poems and rhymes chosen purely for fun and enjoyment. The well-known names, Milligan, Prelutsky, mix with others of an equally irreverent tone.

There is also a lot of fun in the illustrations (as in the original *Giggly Rhymes*) by Julie Park. They extend the poems into an even more fanciful realm. There is so much to look at, so much going on that children will have opportunities to find something new to talk about on every occasion. Some people might be tempted to buy the book just for the illustrations! It would make a good present to share and giggle over.
Age range: 6–9   MM
Theme: Fun

PATTEN, Brian (editor)
Gangsters, Ghosts and Dragonflies
Piper, 1981 (rev. 1993)
152 pp, paperback, ISBN 0–330–32506–X
Contents, Index, b/w line illustrations

There are hints of danger and prickles of fear for the reader who works through this collection of poems for older children. There are also some amazing surprises, one or two unexpected encounters, and occasional off-beat observations. In one poem, James Berry's 'When I Dance', the poet says:

I'm okay at any angle,
Outfit of drums crowds madness round
Talking winds and plucked strings conspire
Beat after beat warms me like the sun

This collections moves through drums and crowds and madness in the same engaging way, and is 'okay at any angle'. It is part of an editor's job, not only to select the right poems but also to place them well, and Patten does this with his mind as well as his ear.
Age range: 12–15   JO
Theme: Crowds, Drums, Madness

PATTERSON, Geoffrey (editor)
Said the Mouse to the Elephant
André Deutsch, 1992
63 pp, hardback, ISBN 0–590–54024–6
Contents, b/w line illustrations

Geoffrey Patterson is an illustrator who likes poetry. Here he selects his favourite animal poems, and sets off each one with an individual black and white drawing.

The collection is fairly traditional containing, amongst others, poems by Belloc (5), Lear, Chesterton, Rose Fyleman and Yeats. Patterson's illustrations – large, lifelike and generally serious – add to the quaintly old-fashioned feel of the book. Providing your library has copies of other animal anthologies (David Jackson's excellent *Way to the Zoo*, for instance) this volume will make a good addition to primary stock.

Age range: 5–10   JO

PINTER, Harold, ASTBURY, Anthony and GODBERT, Geoffrey (editors)
99 Poems in Translation – An Anthology
Faber and Faber, 1944
150 pp, hardback, ISBN 0–571–16964–3,, £14.99
Series: Poets Format, Contents, Index of translators and first lines, Chronological list of poets

Designed as a companion volume to the same editors' *100 Poems by 100 Poets*, this compact, attractively presented collection (arranged in alphabetical order by author), includes poetry from 7th-century BC Sappho through to the almost immediate present. About 30 countries are represented – with France in pole position followed by Russia and Italy – those three providing almost half of these translated poems. Unfamiliarity with the bulk of languages from which these translations are made (which include, for instance, Native American, Chinese and Hungarian) makes it impossible to reflect on the quality of the poems as translations *per se*. That said, the bulk of what is presented here stands up in its own poetic right. However, in tight-cash times, the appeal of this book to most secondary schools will be understandably and justifiably limited.

Age range: 16+   TD
Themes: Death, Exile, Love, Nature

PIRRIE, Jill (editor)
Apple Fire
Bloodaxe, 1993
128 pp, paperback, ISBN 1–85224–206–X
Contents, Foreword by Edward Blishen, Introduction by editor, b/w line illustrations

This book celebrates some of the best poems written in Jill Pirrie's classes since 1987, illustrated with pictures from the school's art classes. In the introduction Edward Blishen has some wise words to say about this defiantly original teacher of English: 'You can aim to provide it [literacy] through cautious banalities, anaemic exercises, dullnesses and smallnesses of every kind . . . Jill Pirrie works on the perfectly opposite principle: and gives her children by way of literacy a fantastic measure of what makes a poet, and habits of language and outlook that must be grander than they would ever otherwise have been.'

Jill Pirrie's own introduction to this marvellous Bloodaxe collection should be compulsory reading for all those concerned directly, or indirectly, with English teaching. It is worth more than all the thousands of words drafted by committee members searching for a National Curriculum formula. Jill Pirrie knows that when she works with her mixed ability groups in this remote corner of Suffolk, she is dealing with the elusive substance of the human imagination – not turning out six inch nails. How magnificently her children respond. There isn't an assessment procedure available which will tell you how good each young poet is. Strongly – *strongly* recommended for teachers in all phases of the educational system.

Age range: 12–14   JO

PRELUTSKY, Jack (selector)
Illustrated by Marc Brown
The Walker Book of Read-Aloud Rhymes for the Very Young
Walker Books, 1987
98 pp, hardback, ISBN 0–7445–0770–7
Index, Introduction by Jim Trelease, colour illustrations

This book is a delight from beginning to end. It starts with a joyous song and ends with a goodnight prayer and has everything in between! There's good language, lively illustration, imagination, magic and a look at all the things that interest the very young – other children, food, pretending, dragons and much more. Children will relate to these poems and see themselves in many of them.

The last paragraph of Jim Trelease's introduction is worth remembering: 'Unlike the toys we buy our children, poems cannot break. Their flavour will last longer than a hundred boxes of sweets. They come already assembled and need only one battery – a reader connected to one child. And that reader can start a glow that lasts a lifetime.'

Age range: 3–8   WEC

PRELUTSKY, Jack (editor)
The Walker Book of Poetry for Children
Walker Books, 1985
245 pp, hardback, ISBN 0–7445–0224–1
Index of titles, of authors, of first lines, of subjects, and sepia colour/line illustrations

The book boasts 572 poems to suit every child's every taste! It contains traditional and very well known poems and also includes work from more modern poets. It is conveniently arranged in thematic sections, although some poems seemed to have wandered (what, for example, are Martin Luther King and George Washington doing in 'Seasons'?). Every section is introduced with a poem by the compiler, Jack Prelutsky.

There are poems for every occasion during the year, for every phase of growing up, nature, nonsense, sadness, humour and many more.

The illustrations by Arnold Lobel are lively and, whether in colour or sepia, are highly appropriate. A full and varied collection, accessible for all children.

Age range: 5–11   MM

Themes: Animals, Children, Cities, Food, Home, Magic, Nature, People, Seasons

PRELUTSKY, Jack (editor)
For Laughing Out Loud
Red Fox (Random House), 1994 (this edition)
84 pp, paperback, ISBN 0–09–923731–8
Thematic, Index of titles, of authors, colour line illustrations

This is a collection of very silly poems which also happen to be very funny. Children of all ages will enjoy the nonsense. Some of the funniest are anonymous, although Ogden Nash is well represented. The use of rhyme, strong rhythm and alliteration make many of the poems easy for children to memorise and chant, which is an essential part of the fun. Some poems are especially good for reading out loud to children, particularly the semi-tongue twisters, for example 'Brother' (Mary Ann Hoberman).

The range of subjects which are objects of fun is impressive and include boys, girls, animals, ghosts and witches.

Illustrations by Marjorie Priceman are colourful, lively and most appropriate for the subject matter.

Age range: 5–9   MM

Theme: Humour

R

RICHARDSON, Polly (editor)
Illustrated by Meg Rutherford

Animal Poems
Simon and Schuster, 1992
32 pp, paperback, ISBN 0–7500–1059–2
Contents, Thematic, colour illustrations

A lovely picture book of animal poems, good to read aloud to the very young. The book moves from tigers to mice on to guinea pigs and kangaroos and to all kinds of creatures. The poems are sometimes descriptive and sometimes just fun as in 'Geraldine Giraffe' which has one word to a line and is as tall as the giraffe by its side; it begins: 'the longest ever woolly scarf was worn by Geraldine Giraffe'. There are poems by Eleanor Farjeon, Dick King-Smith, Jack Prelutsky, Robert Louis Stevenson, Grace Nichols and many other well-known and less well-known poets.

Age range: 4–7   WEC

Theme: Animals

ROBERTS, Michael (editor), revised by PORTER, Peter

The Faber Book of Modern Verse
Faber and Faber, 1936
432 pp, paperback, ISBN 0–571–18017–5
Contents, List of poets, Introduction to the First Edition by Michael Roberts, Introduction to the Fourth Edition by Peter Porter

Faber say this will be the final edition of *The Book of Modern Verse*. The original edition, edited by Michael Roberts in 1936, was revised in 1951 and again in 1965. Peter Porter has made the last revision to the collection and has included the work of 24 new poets. In his short introduction Porter says he has 'chosen to extend the line of modernity in only one direction – towards poetry as fiction, poetry as verbal and philosophical speculation', and has 'preferred to keep the text in one, continuous, unfolding line'. Starting with Hopkins, Yeats, Pound and Eliot, and ending with Plath, Heaney, Dunn and Fenton, this is still the most influential, balanced and appealing representation of modern poetry, both for students and general readers.

The first editor, Michael Roberts, was an inspirational teacher, a fine amateur mountaineer and a poet with a distinctive voice. He died not long after the Second World War, and this fourth edition of his collection is a fitting tribute to a man with a passion for people and poetry.

Age range: 15+   JO

ROBERTS, Susan (editor)

Welcome To The Party

BBC Children's Books, 1993

160 pp, paperback, ISBN 0–563–36482–3, £3.99

Contents, Index of poets, of poems, b/w illustrations

This is a collection of about 125 poems from the BBC's 'Talking Poetry' series, with material in evidence from living writers such as John Agard, Brea Lee, James Berry, Grace Nichols and Philip Gross as well as Scott, Shakespeare, Wordsworth, Hopkins *et al*. The book itself is divided into ten themed sections, such as War, School, Birth and Death, each with its own brief introduction. There is an appealing variety of moods. There is verse rhyming, verse free, verse joyful, verse melancholy, verse light, verse weighty. Given all this variety and such a range of themes, it is not unreasonable to suggest that the most rabid poemophobe ought to find something here to give happy interest.

Age range: 12–16+   TD

Themes: Birds, Birth, Celebration, Cities, Colours, Death, Heroes/Heroines, School, Travel, War, Weather

ROSEN, Michael and STEELE, Susanna (editors)

Inky Pinky Ponky

Picture Lions, 1982

26 pp, paperback, ISBN 0–00–663612–8, £3.99

Line colour illustrations

The special attraction of this paperback edition of *Inky Pinky Ponky* lies in the design. Dan Jones has produced a wonderfully vigorous collection of illustrations, many of them featuring well known London sights and all of them redolent with the multi-ethnic bustle of the big city. The rhymes are fitted below, around, in between, and on top of the pictures, which all adds to the sense of fun and makes this collection a good buy at, £3.99.

Age range: 3–6   JO

S

SAVILLE, Malcolm (editor)

Words for All Seasons

Lutterworth Press, 1979

192 pp, hardback, ISBN 0–7188–2393–1

Contents, Thematic, Index of titles, of authors, of first lines, b/w line illustrations

This collection has a distinctly 'English' feel to it, dealing as it does with traditional festivals and the beauties of the changing seasons. A glance at the index shows that Saville's favourite sources are Anon, the Bible and Christina Rossetti, followed closely by Edward Thomas, Charles Causley, John Clare, Alison Uttley and Mary Webb. The tone is Christian and the poetry, with an odd exception, is lyrical, concentrating on the way the singing tones of poetry can be related to an inspiriting sense of religious observance.

Within the boundaries which he sets, this is a collection which reflects the ideas and attitudes of the editor. It may well appeal to those schools who wish to represent similar approaches and, certainly, contains many fine poems 'for all seasons'.

Age range: 10–16   JO

Theme: The Seasons

SMITH, Janet Adam (editor)
The Faber Book of Children's Verse
Faber and Faber, 1953
412 pp, paperback, ISBN 0–571–05457–9
Contents, Thematic, Index

There is some great stuff in this anthology which has, deservedly, been in print since 1953. Forty years on, the book looks dated – the cover offers little appeal to secondary school students and the layout, typeface and general design are not inviting. This is a selection for the student who already loves poetry and has experience of reading lots of it, not a book to entice a new reader into poetry. From the first poem, by O. StJ. Gogarty, beginning:

> What should we know
> For better or worse
> Of the Long Ago
> Were it not for Verse . . .

there is much to amuse, sadden and delight for those who are willing to ignore appearance and give the contents a chance.
Age range: 9–16+   WEC

W.H. SMITH Young Writers' Judges
Walk the High Wire
MacMillan, 1995
Paperback, ISBN 0–333–62755–5
Contents

When 65 children, from schools all over the country, write as well as this, we should ask ourselves what sort of teaching they are receiving and what kind of rich experiences produce writing of such quality.

> She's the director, the head, the boss,
> Although her toast is burnt
> And baked beans lumpy
> As mushy swamp water.
> She sits in her favourite chair,
> And holds you with the glittering
> Blue eyes of the Ancient Mariner.
> Peering through the gold rings of intelligence,
> Balanced on a small stub nose
> Above two pink lips,
> Which took us to different worlds,
> From that old pink sofa.
> I was there when the Highwayman
> Met his grizzly end,
> When the Ancient Mariner
> Was telling his story,
> When Laura went to the Goblin Market
> And the Lady of Shalott's
> Magic mirror finally cracked.
> This character in patchwork coat,
> Red shoes and long, coloured scarf,
> Would entwine me in all these stories.

She who doted over her old films,
And *film noir* books.
She gave me the confidence
To walk the high wire.

Zoë Brigley, aged 13, wrote the 'Poetry Magician', from which the W.H. Smith collection takes its name. A marvellous book for parents, teachers, children and all those people who devise National Curriculum texts and assignments.

Age range: 5–16+   JO

SNEVE, Virginia (editor)
Dancing Teepees
Oxford University Press, 1989
32 pp, hardback, ISBN 0–19–279881–2
Contents, line colour illustrations

There are some books which need a separate, geographical space in order that they can show themselves to the passing crowd. This is one such volume.

Virginia Sneve has selected from the oral tradition of the North American Indian, and the work of tribal poets, to give us a fascinating glimpse of a complex and poetic native culture.

The poems deal with the lives of the Indians, focusing particularly on their customs and rites. A distinguished American artist, Stephen Gammell, brings the words to life most beautifully, drawing on traditional craft patterns and motifs. The subtle colours, reproduced on high quality paper, make this a very special book at a very affordable price.

Age range: 7–12   JO
Theme: North American Indians

SOMMERVILLE, Rowena (compiler and illustrator)
Don't Step on that Earwig
Red Fox (Random House), 1993
78 pp, paperback, ISBN 0–09–927441–8
Contents, Thematic, b/w illustrations

Poems that concentrate on those things that children love – or hate! There are ants, earwigs, spiders, termites, worms, beetles and many more creepy crawlies, as well as more attractive creatures like butterflies, to read about in this collection. The engaging black and white illustration bring out the humour and mood of the poems. A good book for young readers to dip into.

Age range: 7–12   WEC
Theme: Insects

STEELE, Susanna and STYLES, Morag (editors)
Mother Gave a Shout
A & C Black, 1990
128 pp, hardback, ISBN 0–7136–3242–9, £7.95
Section Contents, Index of poems and poets, of traditional poems, b/w illustrations

Illustrated with effective black and white simplicity by Jane Ray, this is a well-presented anthology of poems by women and girls. It draws upon material old and new from all over the world. Of the 89 poems by known writers, about half-a-dozen are by children, including a most affecting piece from a 1944 concentration camp. In addition there are 20 or so traditional poems – also gathered from far and wide. There is nothing shrill here. Instead there is an engaging mix of moods, material and perspectives in the book's nine sections. Both long and short poems amuse, entertain or provoke thought. There is a useful range of verse forms both rigid and relaxed. The different approaches to language can only help to extend and enrich children's own use of language; they can only grow in language awareness through such happily diverse encounters.

Age range: 8–13+   TD

Themes: Domestic life, Family, Lullabies, Nature, Society, Women in Society

STYLES, Morag (editor)
You'll Love This Stuff!
Poems from many cultures

Cambridge University Press, 1986
112 pp, paperback, ISBN 0–521–31275–2
Sections Contents, Thematic, Indexes of countries and of poems and poets by nationality, Glossary, b/w line illustrations

This anthology contains poems from 44 different countries or cultures. A similar wide range of poets is presented; traditional, modern (and many child poets).

The poems give children opportunities to experience different realities and lifestyles of other people and the natural habitats and lives of animals. An extra delight is descriptions of mangoes and pawpaws, sun-ripe and ready for eating – a long cry from the supermarket!

There is a useful index of countries and the poems plus a glossary of Caribbean dialect so that children can obtain meaning as well as fun from the poems they read. The illustrations by Bernard Georges are varied in style and are well suited to the poems. Children will 'love this stuff'.

Age range: 8–12   MM

Themes: Babies, Play, School, Water, Wildlife

STYLES, Morag and COOK, Helen (editors)
Ink-Slinger

A & C Black, 1990
60 pp, hardback, ISBN 0–7136–3320–4, £6.95
Index of titles, b/w illustrations

Well-supported by Caroline Holden's simple black and white illustrations, there are 52 poems of varying length (mainly short) in this collection. There are poems old, poems new, poems by 'young persons', poems from far-flung corners of the globe. There is the familiar and the strange – all with a focus on the act and craft of writing. There is the formal and the free.

An engaging and thought-provoking volume, this will give pleasure to eager young readers. It may well also serve discreetly an important pedagogical purpose by encouraging them to enjoy writing.

Age range: 10–13+   TD

Theme: Writing

STYLES, Morag (editor)
I Like That Stuff

Cambridge University Press, 1984
96 pp, paperback, ISBN 0–521–27637–3
Contents, Thematic, Index of poets, Glossary, b/w illustrations

This anthology deserves a place in every primary and lower secondary school classroom.

It is still as fresh and exciting as when it was first published. Morag Styles has chosen a wide range of poetry by established poets like John Agard, Grace Nichols and James Berry and by young poets around the world. Some poems are fun and straightforward, others are thought-provoking and challenging in terms of both content and style. There are ballads, haiku, traditional verses, free verse and throughout an emphasis on the rhythms and music of language.

From Edward Kamau Braithwaite's introduction to the final piece by Rabindranath Tagore this is a book to encourage freedom in writing and to widen children's horizons. Listening to the poems is to experience the power and possibilities of words.

Age range: 8–12   WEC

Theme: Multi-cultural verse

W

WADE, Barrie (collator)
Jingle Jangle
Nelson, 1986
48 pp, paperback, ISBN 0–17–413053–8
Series: Story Chest, Colour illustrations

A super collection of playground rhymes to chant and skip to – and to make adults feel nostalgic. All the old favourites are there, not always quite the same as remembered from childhoods in other parts of the country, but as much fun as ever. The book is illustrated in full colour by many illustrators and so every rhyme has its own style and turning the page is very exciting as there's no way to guess what may come next.

Age range: 3–7   WEC

Theme: Playground rhymes

WADE, Barrie (editor)
Poets of the Century
Nelson, 1989 (this edition)
Contents, Notes on poems

Inevitably a book cannot contain all the poets of the century, but the nine poets chosen for this anthology have both stature and appeal. The chosen nine – Yeats, Eliot, Owen, Lawrence, Auden, Larkin, Hughes, Plath and Heaney – give a wide range of moods, themes and topics in their poetry.

Each poet has an introduction which contains relevant events and comments about the poet's life and work, including some comments about poems in the selection. An introduction to the book offers notes to the student about reading and appreciating poetry, together with a warning that not all poetry is immediately or completely understood. The book concludes with notes for the student which may assist some of the understanding.

A very useful book for the classroom teacher and for students to learn to appreciate and respond to poetry from poets who are worth reading. An excellent introduction to some poets of this century.

Age range: 12–16+   MM

Themes: Age, Nature, Relationships, Violence, War

WATERS, Fiona (editor)

Golden Apples

Heinemann, 1985, re-issue 1993
118 pp, hardback, ISBN 0–434–96391–7
Contents, Index, b/w illustrations

Fiona Waters has made a choice of poetry that has something for everyone. There are some unusual choices for a children's anthology ('Stop all the Clocks, Cut off the Telephone' – Auden) but they are some of the many poems in the book that engage the reader's emotions. The balance of poems will engage children at many levels; poems that encourage laughter and empathy, for example, 'Hugger Mugger' by Kit Wright and 'Aunt Julie' by Norman MacCraig. (Everyone has an aunt who bestows wet kisses.) Other poems explore the possibilities of an uncertain future, for example, 'Junk' by Vernon Scannell, which will encourage children to speculate.

The book includes many favourite (Ahlberg), traditional (Yeats, Walter de la Mare) and unexpected (Sylvia Plath, Stevie Smith) poets.

The drawings by Alan Mark complement the poems and do not intrude into the text.

A lovely selection for use in the classroom (and as a present for oneself).

Age range: 8–12   MM

WATERS, Fiona (editor)

Out of the Blue
(An Anthology of Weather Poems)

Young Lions (HarperCollins), 1982, 4th impression 1992
96 pp, paperback, ISBN 0–00–671960–0
Contents, Index, b/w illustrations by Veroni

About 60 poems are packed into this brief, well-presented space, their moods, styles and shapes reflecting well the weather variations the anthology seeks to encapsulate. Familiar, long-established poets and poems co-exist happily with those less well known to make for a delightful, poetry–supportive collection quietly graced by Veroni's neat black and white illustrations. Over 10 years old now, Fiona Waters's anthology continues to have the right to a happy place in both primary and secondary school libraries.

Age range: 10–13   TD
Theme: Weather

WILDSMITH, Brian (illustrator)

Mother Goose – A Collection of Nursery Rhymes

Oxford University Press, 1964
80 pp, paperback, ISBN 0–19–272180–1
Index, colour illustrations

Brian Wildsmith has an extraordinary sense of colour and his brilliantly patterned paintings of people, buildings and scenes give children lots to think about as they read, or listen to, these popular nursery rhymes. There are over 80 rhymes in this collection which, although now 20 years old, looks as fresh as ever. The rhyme, rhythm, repetition and story in these traditional rhymes make them an important element in a young child's life, in learning how to listen and how stories work. Every nursery, infant and junior school class, and every home, should have a Mother Goose collection.

Age range: 2–7   WEC
Theme: Nursery rhymes

WILLIAMS, Sarah (editor)
Ride a Cock Horse
Oxford University Press, 1986
48 pp, paperback, ISBN 0–19–272284–0
Contents, Thematic, colour line illustrations

Already a popular book with parents, and those concerned with the welfare of babies, *Ride a Cock Horse* is now in its ninth reprint. It is a deserved success.

The book is neatly divided into four sections beginning with knee-jogging rhymes (like, 'This is the Way the Lady rides') followed by bouncing and dancing rhymes ('Dance to Your Daddy', for example) moving on to patting and clapping rhymes (such as 'Diddle Diddle Dumpling') and ending with lullabies and rocking rhymes (like, 'Bye Baby Bunting').

Ian Beck finds a perfect style of illustration to match these simple but treasured rhymes which ought to be part of the entitlement of every child in the first years of life. A cassette is also available.

Age range: 0–5   JO

Themes: Bouncing rhymes, Dancing rhymes, Knee-jogging rhymes, Lullabies, Patting and clapping rhymes, Rocking rhymes

WILLIAMS, Sarah (collator)
Illustrated by Ian Beck
Pudding and Pie
Oxford University Press, 1989
48 pp, paperback, ISBN 0–19–272283–2
Series, Contents, colour illustrations

A collection of well-known nursery rhymes presented with lots of magic, wit and imagination. The book is stylish and the rhymes are arranged with care, from the opening 'Boys and girls come out to play' to the final four rhymes, 'Wee Willie Winkie', 'The man in the moon', 'Hey, diddle, diddle' and 'How many miles to Babylon?', all referring to the moon or the end of the day. Ian Beck's animals, appearing on many pages, are wonderful – particularly Old Mother Hubbard's dog, seen reading the 'Dog Times'. This collection is a good introduction to many well-loved nursery rhymes.

A cassette is available to accompany this book.

Age range: 2–6   WEC

Theme: Nursery rhymes

WILLIAMS, Sarah (collator)
Illustrated by Ian Beck
Round and Round the Garden
Oxford University Press, 1983
48 pp, paperback, ISBN 0–19–272282–4
Series, Contents, colour illustrations

A collection of traditional play rhymes – some, like 'Incy, wincy spider' and 'I'm a little teapot', very well known, others certainly new to me. The illustrated instructions at the bottom of each page show the movements clearly. Ian Beck's warm and humorous illustrations bring the rhymes to life. This book is a must for playgroups, nursery and infant classrooms as it contains lots of action rhymes that teachers may have forgotten, or never known.

A cassette is available to accompany this book.

Age range: 2–6   WEC

Theme: Action rhymes

WOOLGER, David (editor)

Who Do You Think You Are?

Poems About People

Oxford University Press, 1990
128 pp, hardback, ISBN 0–19–276074–2, £8.95
Contents, Thematic, Index, b/w line illustrations

An imaginative and far-ranging collection of poems about people. It is tempting to read all of the poems at one sitting, although it is considerately sectioned for short breaks.

The selection covers a wide range of ages, poets and themes. There are 'factual' poems about the body's composition ('Who do you think you are? – Carl Sandberg) plus the mystery of its assembly. Other poems explore the mystery of the mind; dreaming (Robert Graves), thinking (Miroslav) and remembering.

More importantly, perhaps, the poems search cycles and relationships; the cycle of youth and age (for example, Seamus Heaney's 'Follower').

The poems are sensitively chosen, which gives readers of any age a chance to explore different perspectives about different people. In this way they all give opportunity for reflection. It is not a 'light' collection but does contain humour and such delights as 'On Making Tea' (R.L. Wilson), and 'Mrs Reece Laughs' (Martin Armstrong) which then highlight the poignancy of 'When I am Dead' (trad. Indian) or 'Childhood' (Frances Cornford).

The carefully drawn illustrations complement the poems. Those which introduce a section frequently make visual reference to more than one poem – it's fun looking out for them.

Age range: 10+   MM

Theme: People

WOOLGER, David (editor)

The Magic Tree

Oxford University Press, 1981
160 pp, paperback, ISBN 0–19–276046–7
Contents, Thematic, Index, b/w line illustrations

These poems of fantasy and mystery have been collected by David Woolger for secondary pupils and include a number of unexpected and surprising pieces, as well as many traditional old favourites.

The poems are grouped in subsections – Visitors, Transformations, Ghosts, Music, The Sea, and so on – and a different artist provides illustrations for each one.

This is a useful collection to have in the classroom, either for general reading or for those occasions when pupils are preparing poems for group presentation.

Age range: 11–16+   JO

Theme: Creatures, Ghosts, Journeys, Magic, Music, Royal persons, The Sea, Visitors

Poetry Resource Books

A

ABBS, Peter and RICHARDSON, John
The Forms of Poetry
(A Practical Study Guide for English)
Cambridge University Press, 1990, this reprint 1992
216 pp, paperback, ISBN 0–521–37160–0
Contents, Index of poets, Glossary of terms, b/w photographs and line illustrations

Although this guide to the study of poetry is directed at students (as is apparent through the series of commands such as 'Write an essay', 'Make your own study', 'Invent your own form', 'Find five words', 'Experiment', 'Design a poster', 'Read', etc.) the key intention is surely to offer aid, comfort and a range of poetry-teaching strategies to teachers. Of its kind, the book is largely refreshing. There is a chapter which seeks to illustrate something of the symbolic nature of poetry. There is material on form, on perception, on response. The battery of ideas on writing, talking and thinking about poetry seems inexhaustible. The many various kinds of poetry are explored – with legions of lively and interesting examples. In a way, the very fecundity of the book might be off-putting to some students. On the other hand, it stands as a most useful resource book for the hard pressed secondary school teacher.

Age range: 12–16+ TD
Theme: Poetry Study Guide

ALCORN, Maureen and EBBORN, Amanda (editors)
Squeeze Words Hard
Longman, 1990
224 pp, paperback, ISBN 0–582–05059–6
Contents, b/w line illustrations, Assignments after each section

If GCSE means Generally Committing the Same Errors, this collection falls into the trap. There are too many joky poems; too many with a transparent message to deliver; too many chummy, easy-to-get-on-with poems and not enough that startle, sizzle, challenge, sing, puzzle, delight – and demand to be read and re-read.

Of course, there are poems which deserve to be included (but many of these are well known pieces which have regular coverage in other anthologies) and poets whose worth would never be questioned. But the very best anthologies do more than bind poems together in sections labelled, 'Generations Apart', or, 'Nine to Five' – they have a unity and coherence which happens because each poem is comfortable with its neighbours and happy with the particular space it occupies.

And, oh, the interminable exercises, with assignments for absolutely everything. As Edward Blishen said, elsewhere, most of these are 'cautious banalities, anaemic exercises, smallnesses and dullnesses'. Beware!

Age range: 14–16   JO

B

BARLOW, Adrian (editor)
The Calling of Kindred
Cambridge University Press, 1993
174 pp, paperback, ISBN 0–521–44774–7
Contents, Index of first lines, Notes (44 pp) on poets and poems

Adrian Barlow describes his collection as 'a mixture of the well-known and familiar, poems chosen because I have found them memorable'. The volume is arranged in five sections, not according to themes but because the compiler senses links and relationships between the poems in each section. The reader is left to make whatever connections he/she wishes to see.

There are intriguing juxtapositions to contemplate. John Lyly sits next to Primo Levi; Arthur Yap is alongside Blake and Basil Bunting nudges up against Emily Brontë. And there are pleasurable discoveries to be made – Alison Croggan on childbirth, domestic issues and writing poetry, followed immediately by Heng Siok Tian reflecting on how words can be scrabbled and snatched at so hastily that they suffocate.

This is a rich, eclectic gathering. It would have been better without the didactic set of notes, but is, notwithstanding, a welcome addition to the poetry resources for older pupils.

Age range: 14+   JO

BAYLEY, P.C. (editor)
Spenser, The Faerie Queene, Book 1
Open University, published by Oxford University Press, 1966
344 pp, paperback, ISBN 0–19–911011–5
Series: O.U. Set Book, Contents, Introduction, Table of dates, Note on text, Dedication, Notes, Glossary, b/w line illustrations

In Victoria's reign, copies of *The Faerie Queene*, suitably doctored, were to be found in almost every nursery and classroom. Nowadays most adult readers are deterred by the length and complexity of this Romantic narrative with its unfamiliar syntax and Latinate construction.

For the advanced student this O.U. text is a most helpful guide. P.C. Bayley provides a lucid introduction which outlines, briefly, the biographical details of Spenser's life, considers the models and influences of epic and romance forms, and investigates the techniques adopted by the poet. A short, but equally useful section by Alan Ward indicates the major ways in which language was used by Spenser, and this is followed by a table of important dates.

There are extensive notes at the back of the book on the poem and the twelve cantos followed, finally, by a rough guide to meaning in the form of a glossary. This is a book for the serious student. It contains no exercises, no methodological suggestions, no short cuts to understanding, but, like most O.U. texts, has been prepared with sound scholarship and thoroughness.

Age range: 16+ JO

BLEIMAN, Barbara (editor)
Five Modern Poets
Longman
174 pp, paperback, ISBN 0–582–09713–4
Series: Longman Literature, Contents, About the poets, Working on a Poet, Glossary, Working on the Anthology

There are some excellent features about this collection: the chosen poets have vigorous and distinctive voices; the poems range from the gritty and critical to the amusing and restrained; the explored themes and ideas have a strong contemporary feel and the study methods offered to students are imaginative and challenging.

Each of the poets – Adcock, Fanthorpe, Stevenson, Harrison and Walcott – is given a one-page sketch outlining background, experience and achievement, and there is a useful glossary providing brief explanations of the cultural, historical and literary references in the poems.

As well as containing good ideas for individual and group assignments the section called 'Working on the Anthology' reprints a number of interesting reviews of each of the poets. *Five Modern Poets* is strongly recommended, not only for those concerned with teaching advanced students but for all teachers keen to develop their strategies and understanding.

Age range: 16+ JO

C

COOK, Helen and STYLES, Morag
Cambridge Poetry Box: Teacher's Book
Cambridge University Press, 1991
48 pp, paperback, ISBN 0–521–42311–2
Series: covers the Cambridge Poetry Box anthologies, Contents, Glossary, Bibliography

In an ideal world there would be no need for this slim book which is designed to aid teachers using the three Cambridge Poetry Boxes. The jacket lays out its intention of: outlining the principles underlying group readings; suggesting collaborative poetry activities; offering advice on developing children's critical skills; meeting National Curriculum English demands. The book does so in businesslike fashion and offers aid and comfort especially to the non-specialist teacher of the subject. Its bibliography is especially useful. There is distinctly practical advice on: how to select groups; the importance of teacher's own engagement; the learning of reading; approaches to be adopted with the various poems in the anthologies. For those teachers whose poetry insecurity is neurotically pronounced, there are even suggestions as to the questions children might be asked about particular poems. This is a remarkably well-designed poetry crutch!

Age range: 6–12 TD
Theme: Teaching poetry

COOK, Helen and STYLES, Morag (editors)
There's a Poet Behind You
A & C Black, 1988
128 pp, hardback, ISBN 0–7136–3056–6
Contents, Notes on the poets, b/w line illustrations, b/w photographs

If you listened to everything this book tells you about poetry, poets and writing poetry, you might become a poet yourself and change your name to Gimi Jograd, which is the name you get if you put together the first two letters of the forenames of the poets who write in this book. And then you might write a poem yourself:

> Seeing this book is better than hearing about it;
> Opening this book is better than seeing it;
> Reading this book is better than opening it.
> Borrowing this book is better than not having it;
> Buying this book is better than borrowing it;
> Owning this book means something special.
> So borrow it – or buy it,
> Open it – and read it,
> I'll bet you enjoy it.

Age range: 7+   JO
Theme: Reading and writing poetry

CORBETT, Pie and MOSES, Brian
Catapults and Kingfishers
Oxford University Press, 1986
112 pp, paperback, ISBN 0–19–919069–0
Contents, Book list, Recommended anthologies

There are many good ideas packed into this book, all of them based on the authors' considerable experience both as classroom teachers and leaders of teachers' workshops.

The long introduction offers advice on: collage poems; using real poems as models; stimuli and the place of discussion; and the processes of writing poetry, much of it usefully illustrated by work from children.

The main body of the book consists of stages which, the authors say, should not necessarily be used as a scheme. These stages are roughly progressive offering more challenging and complex work towards the end and contain lots of good suggestions for classroom work.

Used in conjunction with books like *Poetry in the Making* (Hughes) and *On Common Ground* (Pirrie), this volume will help all those primary teachers who wish to develop the range of their methodology.

Age range: 5–10   JO

D

DARBISHIRE, Helen (editor)
Wordsworth – Prelude I, II etc
Oxford University Press, First edn. 1928, this edn. 1991
76 pp, paperback, ISBN 0–19–831931–2
Introduction, Notes

This small volume was first published in 1928 (when Huddersfield Town won the championship) and has been reprinted eighteen times – a tribute to its compactness and unadorned style.

Helen Darbishire in the introduction gives a short but insightful account of the poet's life, and his favourite aspiration – to write.

'. . . some philosophic song
Of truth that cherishes our daily life;

With meditations passionate from deep

Recesses in man's heart'

The text printed in this edition is that which Wordsworth agreed with his executors and was eventually published in 1850, after his death. It includes Books I and II, and parts of V and XII. There are 14 pages of helpful notes, following on from the great poem.

Age range: 16+   JO

DAVIES, Walford (editor)
Collected Poems: Dylan Thomas
Everyman; J.M. Dent 1988, this edn. 1994
268 pp, paperback, ISBN 0–460–87369–5
Series: Everyman Library, Contents, Index, Brief chronology, Preface, Notes

The poems collected for this edition are those which Thomas chose for the first publication in 1952, plus two poems that he was working on up to the year of his death. The publisher's claim that this is a definitive edition is reinforced by excellent, scholarly notes which include comments by Thomas himself. It is refreshing to find such detailed notes, helpful and enabling, rather than didactic and prescriptive.

Perhaps the best advice for students studying the work of Dylan Thomas comes from the poet himself. When analysing his own faults (immature violence, rhythmic monotony, overweighted imagery) he suggests: '. . . every line is meant to be understood: the reader is meant to understand every poem by thinking and feeling about it, not by sucking it through his pores'.

For advanced students and aficionados.

Age range: 16+   JO

F

FRY, Don and TORBE, Mike (editors)
Poetry Readings
Hodder and Stoughton, 1993
152 pp, paperback, ISBN 0–340–58841–1
Contents, introduction, b/w line illustrations and photographs

The editors have collected some first-rate material here to form 20 units of study. Each unit consists of a core poem with exploratory work, a short anthology, and suggestions for assignments. Sometimes the poems in the anthology section are by the poet who wrote the core poem: in other units different poets make a contribution.

The strength of this collection lies in the variety and quality of the core poems – Edward Thomas, Tony Harrison, Hardy, Tennyson and Heaney, for instance – and the excellent choices of poems to accompany them. There is an informed, imaginative presence in the editing of this book and (an unusual bonus this) the black and white photographs and drawings add to the overall quality.

There is an 'if only . . .'

If only the assignments had been relegated to the back pages and condensed to exemplars. Most English teachers enjoy devising assignments, often in cooperation with their students, and do not wish to be relegated to the role of administrator. Nevertheless, this collection is so good it should be bought in by English departments which don't already have copies.

Age range: 14+   JO

G

GREEN, Veronica (editor)
Rhythm of Our Days
Cambridge University Press, 1991
136 pp, paperback, ISBN 0–521–38774–4
Contents, Notes on poems and poets

Veronica Green's compilation, *Rhythm of Our Days*, is described as an anthology which reveals the variety and range of voices in women's poetry. The writers represented here were all born in the 20th century and come from a dozen different countries. The poems, which have all been written since the 1950s, reflect the many cultures and issues which are of concern to women poets.

The anthology confirms the enormous strength and quality of women's writing, and even the most casual of browsers will be caught up by the power and eloquence of much of the writing. There are poems about work and love and friendship; about white liberals, physical violence, and betrayal; there are funny poems and sad poems; poems to sponsor both wonder and anger, and poems about poetry and the power of words. There are in fact so many good poems by so many good writers that all young people should have access to at least one copy.

Age range: 14+   JO

GROVES, Paul, GRIFFIN, John and GRIMSHAW, Nigel (editors)
Steps to Poetry
Longman, 1989
144 pp, series paperback, ISBN 0–582–03059–5
Series: Steps: A Basic English Course, Contents, b/w and colour photographs

This is a bright-looking book with over 30 lively photographs and text sometimes on different (i.e. non-white) coloured paper. With about 64 thematically arranged and almost totally 20th-century poems (just over a quarter of them by women), the editors have sought a careful path between the trendy and the traditional. There is a freshness about many of the poems – many of which have not as yet been over-anthologised. There are C.P. Cavafy and Wendy Cope. There are Harrison and Heaney. Milligan sits alongside Mitchell, Agard alongside Pam Ayres – and so on. There are new poets.

The introduction gives guidance on the likely ingredients of poems – Rhythm, Rhyme; on Writing Poetry. It also suggests (dangerously?) 'What to do with a Poem'. In the main body of the text there are Five Steps for each poem – that is, questions for students; statements by the editors; highlighted quotations; personal response suggestions; and, usually, assignments.

It might be thought that the introductory thoughts on poetry are coming rather late for GCSE students. Some will see the steps and the final general assignments as mere pedagogical crutches. However, if there are lame teachers, a copy of this book could be useful. The variety of mood and theme in the poetry itself, the presence of some poems in non-standard English and the unfamiliarity of many of the poems are particular virtues.

Age range: 15+   TD

Themes: Age, The Past, School, Feelings, Environmental issues

H

HADLEY, Helen
Bright Ideas: Inspirations for Poetry
Scholastic Publications, 1992
192 pp, paperback, ISBN 0–590–53009–7
Series: Inspirations, Contents, b/w line illustrations

This book contains a host of ideas to encourage children to use and explore language to help their writing of poetry. The ideas are totally practical for the classroom, including ways of using poetry across the curriculum and different ways of presenting poetry.

The book is divided into chapters (for example, Poetry with Beginners, Oral and Traditional Poetry, Ways of Getting Started) which are themselves subdivided into three sections: aspects which need consideration, issues specific to the topic and practical activities for children's writing or work with poetry. Some of these activities are designed for individuals, pairs, groups or classes. Photocopiable material is also provided.

The book also contains useful references to poems and poets to use as a source and a useful resource section includes Books for Teachers, addresses and Books for Children.

This book should be on every primary teacher's bookshelf.

Age range: Teachers only   MM

Theme: Writing

HARRISON, Michael and STUART-CLARK, Christopher (editors)
Writing Poems
Oxford University Press, first published 1985, this edn. 1994
136 pp, paperback, ISBN 0–19–834270–5
Series: Companion to Poems 1 and Poems 2, Contents, Index, Notes for the teacher, b/w and colour line illustrations, b/w photographs

There have been six reprints of this anthology which was designed to encourage pupils to write poetry themselves. The strength of the book lies in the way these skilled editors combine imaginative, workable ideas for pupils to use, with a splendid collection of poems.

The book opens with some short but useful advice for teachers. It is then organised around the different forms and patterns available to young writers and a set of themes selected to stimulate written work. The follow-up suggestions at the end of each sub-section show how well the editors understand teaching processes. These may be used by pupils working individually, or adapted by the teacher to encourage discussion and interaction.

With lively black and white and colour illustrations, this is an attractive and extremely useful book, which will help teachers at the top end of the primary school, and in the early years at the secondary stage.

Age range: 10–14   JO

HEALY, Maura (editor)

Quartet of Poems

Longman, 1993
156 pp, paperback, ISBN 0–582–08299–4
Contents, Introduction to poets, Notes, Coursework assignments, Wider reading

What a pity this wonderful collection of poetry by four black women poets looks so schoolish when opened. The cover looks good but, inside, the book is more about assignments than enjoyment. However, get rid of that moment of disappointment and there are many wonderful poems to enjoy in this collection. The opening poem, the well-known 'Phenomenal Woman' that Maya Angelou often performs with such power and conviction, sets the tone of the book and fills the reader with expectation. She writes with confidence and anger and really makes words work. There's anger too in some of Alice Walker's poems but there's also great sensitivity, as in 'Poem at Thirty-Nine', in which the poet remembers her father. Grace Nichols also remembers the history of black women. In 'Holding My Beads' she writes of what she seeks: 'the power to be what I am/a woman charting my own future' and her strong, distinctive writing suggests that she has found this power. Her poem 'Beauty', brings in a softer mood which is picked up in some of Lorna Goodison's poems such as 'I Am Becoming My Mother' and 'For My Mother (May I Inherit Half Her Strength)'. This is a positive collection, reflecting the power that can come from struggle; full of history and rhythm.

Age range: 13+   WEC
Theme: Black women poets

HYDES, Jack

Touched With Fire

Cambridge University Press, 1985
207 pp, paperback, ISBN 0–521–31537–9
Contents, Indexes of first lines and poets

Touched With Fire contains a good mix of contemporary and traditional poems which span a range of 400 years and which encompass a variety of styles, topics and moods. The collection would be good for individual reading and class use. It is designed, however, as a teaching text. The individual poems are not annotated but they are organised into 6 sections; small anthologies of 22 poems, each anthology having a mixture of styles and ages. The sections are interspersed with guidance for writing poetry essays and examination answers. Specimen answers are included, some better than others, to enable students to analyse which responses get better marks.

In his introduction, Jack Hyde states that the advantage of a poem is the 'pleasure gained from shared experience'. His choice guarantees that all readers will gain some pleasure from dipping into this book. It has a 'modern' approach which collects poems from many countries: Nigeria, Barbados, USA, Ireland, South Africa, the Gambia, Jamaica, and contains contemporary favourites (McGough), old favourites (John Donne, Robert Browning), and some surprises – Cole Porter!

Age range: 14–16   MM

K

KITCHEN, David (editor)

Thin Ice
Oxford University Press
144 pp, paperback, ISBN 0–19–833183–5
Contents, 14 pages of work suggestions, b/w illustrations

This is a pretty comprehensive collection of about 70 poems, with some attractive, supportive illustrations by three artists. Drawn from several countries, the poems do, however, contain several that are widely familiar (such as 'Ozymandias') and poems by well-established names – including Wordsworth, Shakespeare, Ted Hughes, Shelley, Blake *et al*. That is not a criticism. Indeed, it is good to see them here alongside newer and less well-known names. The volume, as a whole, has variety – provides material narrative, descriptive, amusing and serious, trivial and thought-provoking. The editor's pairing of poems in order to promote discussion and his follow-up suggestions are unobtrusive: they may be useful to a less than confident or non-specialist teacher of the subject.

Age range: 14–16+   TD

Themes: Contrasts, People, Animals, Love, Age, Prejudice, Language

L

LEE, Victor (series editor)

Oxford Student Texts
Oxford University Press
Series: Oxford Student Texts, paperback
Contents, Indexes of first lines and titles, b/w photographs

ANSTEY Sarah

William Wordsworth: Selected Poems
1990 176 pp ISBN 0–19–831951–7

FEENEY, Peter

Gerard Manley Hopkins: Selected Poems
1994 152 pp ISBN 0–19–831961–4

GILL, Richard

W.B. Yeats: Selected Poems
1993 150 pp ISBN 0–19–831966–5

John Donne, Selected Poems
1990 175 pp ISBN 0–19–831950–9

GURR, Elizabeth

Pope: The Rape of the Lock
1990 2nd edition 1992 132 pp ISBN 0–19–831958–4

MACK, Peter
Geoffrey Chaucer: General Prologue to the Canterbury Tales
1994 152 pp ISBN 0–19–831967–3

TODD, Jan
D.H. Lawrence, Selected Poems
1993 184 pp ISBN 0–19–831962–2

WILLMOTT, Richard
Thomas Hardy: Selected Poems
1992 143 pp ISBN 0–19–831963–0

Quite attractively presented, each of the slim texts in this series for students follows, in the main, a common format – the work of the individual poet followed by: Notes; Approaches to Study of the text; a brief reading list; possible follow-up activities; in some cases a chronology; in some cases a few black and white photographs. One or two poems also contain a photocopy of a manuscript.

In brief, none of these study texts is as intimidating as such books can sometimes be. Although there is a degree of 'telling' by each editor, there is less didactiveness than can sometimes infect such series. However, such materials are always to be used sensitively. If they are not, what are intended to become highly motivating learning supports can become plagiaristic crutches.

Age range: 15–18+   TD

M

MAGEE, Wes (editor)
Read a Poem, Write a Poem
Simon and Schuster, 1989
64 pp, paperback, ISBN 0–7501–0440–6
Contents, Thematic, b/w and colour line illustrations

Not only has Wes Magee a sure touch in the selection of poems for this volume, he also knows how to advise and encourage children to read and write poetry.

The collection is divided up into themes – shape poems, talking poems, thin poems, poems about numbers and so on; and each set is followed by a page of suggestions called Your Writing Page. Because Wes Magee understands both poetry and children, the ideas on these pages are concrete, creative and helpful. He provides interesting starting points, suggests ways of developing the writing and is never afraid to reveal the structure behind a poem and offer it as a model to the reader/writer.

Amongst others, Kit Wright, Edwin Morgan, Judith Nicholls, Richard Edwards and Magee himself are featured in this excellent collection. It will prove a valuable resource in primary schools.

Age range: 6–10   JO
Themes: Counting, Sun and Moon, Days and Weeks, Alphabets, Lists

MAGEE, Wes (editor)
Cambridge Contemporary Poets 1
Cambridge Contemporary Poets 2
Cambridge University Press, 1992
127 and 125 pp, paperbacks, ISBN 0–521–39749–9 and 0–521–39750–2
Contents, Indexes of first lines, Creative writing suggestions, b/w line illustrations and photographs

Presumably the beginning of a more extended series, each of these two books contains, as the covers tell us: an autobiographical note on each of the eight contemporary poets represented; a selection from each poet's work; a favourite poem from the past chosen by each poet; and some creative writing suggestions by Wes Magee.

Both volumes are well presented – with photographs of each poet and brief Fact File pen-portraits to supplement the autobiographical sketches. All the 16 poets are high in young people's poetry stakes – and deservedly so. The resulting anthologies provide a most interesting variety of poems in terms of structure, mood, tone and length. Stanley Cook's visual Flower poems are of particular interest. It is interesting also to see the poets' choices of favourite past poems. Wes Magee's pedagogical intentions are properly subservient to his lively approach in presenting these poets as people. Their work is likely to refresh young people.
Age range: 10–13   TD
Themes: Childhood, People, Adolescence

MAGEE, Wes (editor)
Poetry
Scholastic, 1993
192 pp, paperback, ISBN 0–590–53021–6
Series: Scholastic Collections, Contents, Index of themes, of first lines, of poets, b/w line illustrations

This is a comprehensive collection of traditionally classic and contemporary poems, compiled by one of the contemporary poets, Wes Magee.

The poems cover a wide range of topics, sectioned into seven major themes (although a comprehensive theme index covers many more). The first section 'Living on Land' explores homes, creatures and animals including cats (Thomas Hood) and tigers (Blake). 'Where there's Water' makes reference to rain, rivers and the sea (e.g. 'Sea-fever' by Masefield and 'The Owl and the Pussy Cat' by Lear). 'Up and Away' includes 'Windy Night' by R.L. Stevenson and 'The Eagle' (Tennyson) as well as poems about balloons, pilots and astronauts.

'People, People, People' celebrates the differences between people in terms of personality, likes and dislikes and highlights the differences between those who have and those who do not ('Two Boys Crying', Ray Mather).

'The Modern World' has as its primary focus machines and transport (and associated problems) although ailments such as colds and 'Chicken Spots' (Peter Dixon) have a place. 'Crystals' (Barrie Wade), however, evocative of African plains, is peculiarly placed in this section.

'School Days' contains mainly humorous poems about school life. 'From the Classroom Window' (John Walsh) and 'I Hear' (Berlie Doherty), however, take the reader outside the confines of the classroom. 'Through the Year' has poems for each season of the year.

Most sections include extracts from longer poems, for example 'Pied Piper' (Browning), 'The Mermaid' and 'The Merman' (Tennyson), 'Kubla Khan' (Coleridge) and 'The Song of Hiawatha' (Longfellow).

Illustrations by Merida Woodford offer an additional humorous element.

Many of the pages are photocopiable, which makes this anthology an even greater asset for the busy primary teacher.

Age range: 6–11   MM

Themes: Land, Water, People, School

MARKUS, Julia and JORDAN, Paul (editors)
Poems 2
Longman, 1995
176 pp, paperback, ISBN 0–582–25401–9
Series: Longman Literature, Contents, Introduction, Glossary, Technical terms, Study programme

It is usually easy to tell whether the editors of books like this are putting together a collection because they have a genuine concern for poets and poetry, or are cashing in on a need for National Curriculum material. Markus and Jordan clearly care for the texts they have assembled here.

No one could quibble with the choice of poets – Heaney, Fanthorpe, Plath, Angelou, Larkin, Duffy and Stevenson – and the editors have selected about a dozen poems to represent each one. There is a potted biography at the beginning of each section, some good advice about reading poetry and, for those who need someone else's props, the obligatory study programme of assignments.

English departments wanting to introduce youngsters to some of the best modern voices will find this volume, and its companion, *Poems 1*, a useful addition to their stock.

Age range: 15+   JO

MARTIN, Christopher (editor)
Poems in Focus
Oxford University Press, 1985, this 6th printing 1994
192 pp, paperback, ISBN 0–19–831248–2
Contents, Index of first lines, Glossary of technical terms, Notes, Work suggestions, b/w photographs

This is a collection of largely modern and predominantly British verse – written mainly by men. Grouped into themes such as War, The Natural World, Love and Marriage, People, and Reflections, there is a mix of well-anthologised and less well-known material. Sound support comes too from about 15 black and white photographs. Each section ends with largely helpful brief notes and with suggestions for work. The latter include also a battery of comprehension and other questions that are not guaranteed to lead to a liking for poetry – especially if the book falls into careless teacherly hands. There is also on occasion some irritating didacticism that is less than likely to encourage personal response by students. The heavy-booted nature of some of the instructions to students is also noticeable – (e.g. 'Examine the full-stop and line-end pauses', 'Make a list', 'Tell the story'). All this said, there are worthwhile poems here, and the book could be sensitively used.

Age range: 15–16+   TD

Themes: War, WWI, WWII, Natural world, Love, Marriage, Children, Parents, Reflections

MILLGATE, Michael (editor)
Tennyson: Selected Poems
Oxford University Press, 1963
217 pp, paperback, ISBN 0–19–911056–5
Series: New Oxford English, Contents, Introduction, Notes to the poems, Tennyson's life,
Chronology

Carlyle once described Tennyson as 'a fine, large-featured, dim-eyed, bronze-coloured, shaggy-headed man – dusty, smoky, free and easy – a most restful, brotherly, solid-hearted man'. The poet enjoyed a popularity rarely achieved by living writers, and Millgate, in his interesting introduction outlines not only the main events, ideas and beliefs associated with Tennyson, but also offers a balanced critical appreciation.

The selection of poems include all Tennyson's best known works: 'The Lady of Shalott'; 'Break Break, Break'; 'Now Sleeps the Crimson Petal'; 'In Memoriam'; 'The Splendour Falls'; 'The Charge of the Light Brigade' – and are accompanied by 13 pages of helpful notes.

Oxford's English Series – as opposed to their Student Texts – are not weighed down with assignments and tasks and study programmes. Whether you regard this as a positive or negative feature depends on how you view the rôle of the English teacher working with advanced students.

Age range: 16+   JO

MORRIS, Helen (editor and arranger)
The New Where's That Poem?
An Index of Poems for Children
Simon and Schuster, 1992 (4th edn)
244 pp, paperback, ISBN 0–7501–0200–4, £9.99
Contents, Index, List of books referred to

This is a book which ought to be indispensable in all schools. Helen Morris has revised and updated this remarkably helpful reference book now for the fourth time since its first appearance in 1967. Her loving labour works to the advantage of any child or adult who wants or needs to find a poem on a particular topic. The Index moves pretty comprehensively from Aborigines (four references) through Lovers: Unhappy (37 references!) to Zoos (three references). And then comes the index of books plus the index of almost 1,000 poets to whom at least one poem is attributed. It really is a remarkable and happy endeavour.

Age range: 4–16+   TD
Theme: Index of children's poems

O

OWEN, W.J.B. (editor)
Wordsworth and Coleridge: Lyrical Ballads
Oxford University Press, first published 1969, this reprint 1993
180 pp, paperback, ISBN 0–19–911006–9
Series: Oxford Critical Commentaries, Contents, Appendices

P

PRINCE, F.T. (editor)
Milton: Comus and Other Poems

Oxford University Press, first published 1968, this reprint 1990
197 pp, paperback, ISBN 0–19–911025–5
Series: Oxford Critical Commentaries, Contents, Appendices

Each of these Oxford Critical Commentaries has had a long life: the Wordsworth/
Coleridge is in its 16th edition. This book was re-issued in a new edition in 1969 and
later, with corrections, in 1971. The Milton is now in its 7th edition. There is clearly a
scholarly thoroughness about the books. Each contains a substantial introduction which
seeks to set the poet's worth in its historical and biographical context. Each has a
meticulous section of textual commentaries. The Owen volume follows Commentary
with an annotated Appendix to the Preface to the Lyrical Ballads. The Prince volume
also contains an Appendix on Renaissance Platonism and Cosmology and a brief
chronology of Milton's life. In the midst of a sense of academic thoroughness, there are,
perhaps, questions to be asked about the hospitality of these volumes. There is something
clinically severe in their manner of presentation which might tend to leave them idle on
library shelves for longer than they deserve.

Age range: 16+   TD
Theme: Critical commentaries

R

RAMCHAND, Kenneth and GRAY, Cecil (editors)
West Indian Poetry

Longman Caribbean, 1989
238 pp, paperback, ISBN 0–582–76637–0
Contents, Thematic, Index, Introduction, Questions on the poems, List of poems by the
author

There are more than 150 poems in this remarkable collection of Caribbean poetry. Many
names will be familiar to the poetry-reading public in Britain – Edward Braithwaite,
Derek Walcott, James Berry, John Agard, Grace Nichols – but there are many exciting
new voices represented here in a collection which reveals the range, versatility and
richness of West Indian poetry.

The editors are both teachers at the University of the West Indies and it is clear that
this is a textbook for use in preparing pupils for what is known as the CXC examination.
Don't let that deter you. This is a first-rate source book which will repay the keen reader's
interest, and provide excellent material for classroom investigation.

Age range: 15+   JO

S

SANSOM, Peter
Writing Poems
Bloodaxe, 1994
127 pp, paperback, ISBN 0–85224–204–3
Contents, Introduction, Glossary, Bibliography, Useful addresses

Good writers are able to reveal their qualities quickly. At the beginning of this book, Peter Sansom takes a poem by Simon Armitage and, in around 200 words, gives a personal response to it. Pick out the key phrases from this analysis – accurate observation, real detail, plain writing, honest expression, figurative meaning, precision, unsentimental response – and you have Sansom's credo for writing poetry.

But don't stop there. The book is a real treasure chest, not just for aspiring writers but for anyone who wants to know how poetry works and why it is worth reading. And how about these for intriguing sub-headings: Buckets; Reading and Garlic; Shards; Seagulls and Teapots; the Scenic Route; the Disaster Poem.

The trouble with a book like this (trouble?) is that it is too good to put down, and even when the last word has been read it can be revisited with pleasure and profit. If you have a passing interest in poetry put it on your birthday list. If you have a passion for poetry buy it at once.

Age range: 16+   JO

STALLWORTHY, Jon (editor)
The Poems of Wilfred Owen
Chatto and Windus, 1985, 8th impression 1995
200 pp, paperback, ISBN 0–7011–3661–8
Contents, Index, Biographical table, Introduction, Extensive footnotes to each poem

This is a work of love as well as scholarship. In the introduction Stallworthy talks about Owen as 'a ghostly addition to the family', and it is easy to see how his presence intruded into the daily routines of the editor's household. The book includes a detailed biographical table, a short but useful introduction to the poems, and contains the texts of all the finished poems of Owen's maturity, plus twelve fragments. There are notes – often extensive – set below each poem which, typically, provide the reader with information about where and when the poem was written, and furnish pertinent details concerning drafting, substantive variations, titles and revisions.

Stallworthy's poetic imagination makes him an ideal editor for a publication that is essential reading for students of the poetry of the First World War.

Age range: 16+   JO

T

TISSIER, Adrian (editor)
Poems from other Centuries
Longman, 1994
182 pp, paperback, ISBN 0–582–22585–X
Series: Longman Literature, Contents, Thematic, Activities and study questions,
Appendix, b/w line illustrations

Driven by National Curriculum demands, this anthology presents about 85 largely familiar pre-20th-century poems – or extracts from longer poems, grouped broadly thematically. About a quarter of the 40 poets represented are women. Brightened briefly by seven black and white illustrations, this collection usefully succeeds in drawing together a range of material for which busy teachers might otherwise have to hunt through dusty stock cupboards. It is also, incidentally, a firm reminder of some of the classroom problems posed by the National Curriculum insistence on pre-20th-century material.

In a sympathetic endeavour to help less secure teachers and students, there is some straightforward (if sadly belated) advice on 'How To Approach The Poems'. More confident teachers (and students) might, however, feel that both the nature and tone of the advice is patronising.

In addition to brief biographical notes on each poet, glossaries, advice on ready texts, there is also a section given over to activities and study questions. Here, again, there is an odd mix of modern classroom approaches and old-style exam tasks of the 'Discuss, Compare, Comment' kind. Lest this criticism seems mere carping, it has to be said that the book will meet the needs of some secondary school English departments.

Age range: 14–16+ TD

Themes: Love, War, Heroism, Myths and symbols, Nature, Environmental issues, Time, Age and death

W

WALTER, Colin (editor), RICHARDS, Roy (consultant editor)
An Early Start to Poetry
Macdonald Educational, 1989
80 pp, paperback, ISBN 0–356–16046–7
Contents, Index, Bibliography, Teachers' notes, Useful addresses, colour line illustrations

A very varied collection of rhyme and poetry of all kinds by poets old and new and by children. Simple first poems appear alongside demanding pieces, such as extracts from 'The Rime of the Ancient Mariner' and 'The Prelude'.

This is a teachers' book aiming to offer practical help in approaching poetry in the classroom. There's lots of information: a long introduction with some good ideas hidden in it, a bibliography and details of poetry organisations. The book really tries to do too much. We're even assured that the illustrations suggest cross-curricular activities to be developed from the poems. For young children the experience of poetry must be enjoyable and thought-provoking, never heavy and worthy; at times the good ideas and exciting poetry in this book become submerged by the importance of it all.

Age range: 5–11 WEC

WILLMOTT, Richard (editor)
Blake's Songs of Innocence and Experience
Oxford University Press, 1990
147 pp, paperback, ISBN 0–19–831952–5
Contents, Index, Approaches: rhythm and imagery; context; beliefs etc., colour line illustrations

Part of a new series designed to introduce students to the work of great English poets and playwrights, this edition of *Blake's Songs of Innocence and Experience* places the poetry first, 'to stress its importance and to encourage students to enjoy it without secondary, critical material'. Nevertheless, twice the number of pages the poems occupy are given over to explanatory notes, approaches and tasks.

Teachers who need considerable help themselves at an informational and contextual level will find the notes useful and may wish to incorporate some of the assignments into a study programme. More confident, experienced teachers will use the book alongside others which offer insights into Blake's life and work.

Age range: 16+   JO

WILLMOTT, Richard (editor)
Four Metaphysical Poets
Cambridge University Press, 1985
184 pp, paperback, ISBN 0–521–27758–2
Contents, Thematic, Index of first lines, Explanatory notes

This anthology contains poems by Donne, Herbert, Marvell and Vaughan. The poems are arranged in sections by poets and there is a fifth section of 'other poets' which provides poems for comparison; these in the last section are not all metaphysical. Willmott separates the love and religious poems in each of the major sections.

The poems themselves need no comment, except perhaps to state the pleasure that reading them gives.

Willmott however, recognises that much of metaphysical poetry is difficult, particularly when reading it for the first time. He has therefore produced copious notes for each poem.

His own love of the poetry is evident – the notes are painstaking and personal. There are so many, however, that at times the poems are in danger of suffocation through explanation – even for those who wish to study the poetry in detail. However, the notes are almost worth studying in their own right! They are also excellent preparation material for examinations.

An ideal book for secondary school study of the metaphysical poets.

Age range: 11–16+   MM
Theme: Metaphysical poets

WOOD, Lynn and Jeffrey (editors)
(a) # Cambridge Poetry Workshop 14+
Cambridge University Press, 1989, This 3rd printing 1993
140 pp, paperback, ISBN 0–521–33673–2
Series: Modern Poetry, Contents, Index of poets, b/w line illustrations and photographs
(b) # Cambridge Poetry Workshop GCSE
Cambridge University Press, 1988, This 5th printing 1993
167 pp, paperback, ISBN 0–521–33672–4
Series: Modern Poetry, Contents, Index of poets, b/w line illustrations and photographs
(c) # Cambridge Poetry Workshop Keystage 3
Cambridge University Press, 1991
106 pp, paperback, ISBN 0–521–38796–5
Series: Modern Poetry, Contents, b/w line illustrations and photographs

The three well-presented volumes in this Workshop series claim to offer poems which have been 'stimulating and appealing in the classroom'. Each book has a number of thematic units, each with its own Thinking/Talking points and its own creative/critical assignments. Ancient and modern poets are represented throughout – from Shakespeare to the present day. In line with the editors' claims, each contains a substantial sprinkling of the long-familiar – such as Holub's 'Boy's Head', Blake's 'Poison Tree', Noye's

'Highwayman', Shelley's 'Ozymandias' in the 14+ volume; through Frost's 'Out, Out', Heaney's 'Death of a Naturalist', Lawrence's 'Snake', Owen's 'Dulce et Decorum' in the GCSE volume; to Tennyson's 'Brook', Auden's 'What is That Sound?', Belloc's 'Matilda' and Eliot's 'Macavity' in the Keystage 3 volume. The last, briefer and more recent volume, however, does contain rather more signs of attention being paid to the multicultural nature of our society and many of our schools. The real question has to centre on the use to which such a series are put. The danger is that the editors come between student and poem. On the other hand, all three volumes offer possibilities for a less than secure, new or non-specialist teacher of English. The best advice for schools really is not to buy blind whole sets of the series until they have undergone firm classroom tests!

> Age range: (a) 14+
> (b) 15–16+
> (c) 11–13+ TD

WOODHEAD, Chris (editor)
Nineteenth and Twentieth Century Verse
Oxford University Press, 1984, this reprint (7th) 1993
236 pp, paperback, ISBN 0–19–831247–4
Contents, Index of first lines, Glossary, b/w photographs

This is an anthology of the generally most familiar and accessible poems by 16 poets writing in English in the nineteenth and twentieth centuries. All are white; all are male. The work of each poet is introduced by a brief biographical sketch and there are just over 50 pages of notes on the poems, plus a glossary outlining the meanings of nine words such as 'metaphor', 'simile' and 'sonnet'. The notes also contain a number of fairly authoritarian suggestions – 'Compare', 'Think about', 'Read aloud', etc. Moreover, although there are questions which invite individual responses, there is also a regrettably didactic tone to many of the commentary elements. It is possible that this book could offer support to insecure teachers. The more secure would do better to turn to uncontaminated selections of these poets' work.

> Age range: 14–16+ TD

The Poetry Society (editors)
B.P. Teachers' Poetry Resources File for Secondary Schools
The Poetry Society, 1992, with 1993/1994 updates
114 pp, looseleaf in hardback ring binder, ISBN 0–9519368–1–6
Contents, colour line illustrations and photographs

At first sight this looks like a National Curriculum folder. In reality, however, after a brief endorsement by Seamus Heaney, it is an invaluable, easily accessible cornucopia – with the clear possibility of overflow through the helpful looseleaf format. Distinguished names abound – of poets, anthologies, teachers, librarians – all with something powerful to say about poetry and its importance. There are practical suggestions about the making and performing of poetry in and beyond the classroom. With sections in different colours, there are careful guides on inviting poets into schools, on Book Weeks and Poetry Festivals, on Poetry Policy. There are clear pointers to sources of help and to book lists. The fact that National Curriculum English has undergone a change in 1995 does not diminish the value of this excellent, well-presented project. Every secondary school English teacher should have a copy – and use it.

> Age range: 11–16+ TD

B.P. Poetry Resources File for Primary Schools
The Poetry Society, 1992
A file to be added to and updated, hardback, ISBN 0–9519368–0–8
Contents, b/w and colour line illustrations, b/w photographs

This file has been produced by the Poetry Society with sponsorship from British Petroleum. It is arguably the most important addition to teaching resources in recent years for all those concerned with establishing a thriving arts programme in schools.

The file serves many purposes: an excellent storehouse of ideas for classroom work; a reference resource book which covers philosophy as well as practice; a checklist and guide for implementing poetry teaching; a source of information about poets, poetry books and poetry festivals. The ring binder allows up-to-date sections to be added, or current material extracted for use or cross-referencing. Both primary and secondary versions of the file are being produced.

The contributors to the primary file include: Wes Magee, Judith Nicholls, Barrie Wade and Mick Gowar; and, in the updates section: Gillian Clarke, Menna Elfyn and Graham Mort. Seamus Heaney lends weight to the venture: 'It is an important step on the road to a rich and more varied treatment of the art in the classroom. I am greatly impressed by the initiation of the project'.

All schools must buy a copy of this excellent publication

Age range: 5–10   JO

Audio Tapes

AGARD, John
Laughter is an Egg
Collins Audio (HarperCollins Audio), 1993
64min Audio tape, ISBN 0–00–10734–9
Contents and colour photograph (both on tape sleeve)

There are almost 50 poems here 'hatched', as the sleeve says, by John Agard – and performed by him to musical and sound-effect accompaniments, the book of the cassette name first emerging in 1990. There is real life in both the poems and in the poet's versatile representations – some straightforwardly recited, some chanted, some almost sung, all of them feeling the benefit of his gentle Caribbean intonations. Rhythm is happily dominant – as is fun with rhyme. The cassette is perfectly listenable in its own right – but has to be a bonus sitting alongside the text in a happy book or library corner.

Age range: 5–9+   TD
Themes: Humour, Laughter, School, Magic

A Golden Treasury of Nursery Rhymes
Tempo, 1992
Audio tape – 30 nursery rhymes, ISBN 1–86–022022–3
Contents, no illustrations

A pleasant enough tape of traditional nursery rhymes and, once they become familiar, children will enjoy joining in. So much the better though to use one of the many imaginatively illustrated books as an introduction to these well-loved rhymes and so to start young children on the reading journey.

Age range: 2–6   WE
Theme: Nursery rhymes

McGOUGH, Roger
Pillow Talk
HarperCollins Audio, 1993
Audio tape, ISBN 0–00–101733–0

Roger McGough's very familiar and distinctive voice gives extra life to the poems in his collection *Pillow Talk* (Puffin, 1992, ISBN 0–14–032504–2). The poems are fun and full of the kind of word play that children really respond to. The poet's rather understated way of speaking his poems makes the jokes even better. The rather inconsequential music used between groups of poems is irritating and pointless as it seems to be out of keeping with the mood of both the poet and his poetry.

This tape is a useful one to use alongside the book and to bring another voice into the classroom.

Age range: 7+ WEC

One, Two, Buckle My Shoe and Other Favourite Rhymes
Tempo Children's Classics, undated
Audio tape
Contents

There are over 50 nursery rhymes and songs on this tape so all are quite short. Surely it would have been better to include fewer and repeat verses to help children to get to know the rhymes. The style of presentation is rather predictable and not likely to hold young children's attention for very long – the whole tape lasts 48 minutes. Snippets of the tape could work with small groups but it would be much better to use alongside a book.

Age range: 2+ WEC

Theme: Nursery rhymes

PATTEN, Brian

Gargling with Jelly
Collins
Audio tape, ISBN 0–00–101773–X

The joky, irreverent, comic collection of poems, *Gargling with Jelly*, first published in 1985, now has a cassette to go with it. And all the poems presented here by Brian Patten and Shireen Shah, come from that book.

Even though the poet and his helper try hard to infuse humour and life into their presentation, the end result doesn't quite match the gusto and anarchic feel of the book. Poems about green snot, slug and worm jam, see-through stomachs and nose-pickers, have more power when they feature as a shared conspiracy between young readers. The public voice makes them part of the adult world and reduces their power.

In small doses, the cassette will make a useful addition to a well-stocked poetry library.

Age range: 6–9 JO

Poetry Contacts

Arts Councils

Arts Councils have larger responsibilities for funding and organisation. They are useful sources of information particularly of national events. A list of contacts at Arts Councils follows:

Arts Council of England
14 Great Peter Street
London
SW1 P3NQ
Tel: 0171–333–0100
Literature Director: Dr Alastair Niven

Arts Council of Dublin
70 Merrian Square
Dublin 2
Tel: 00353–1–6611840
Literature Officer: Lar Cassidy

Arts Council of Northern Ireland
185 Stranmillis Road
Belfast
BT9 5DU
Tel: 01232–381591

Literature and Traditional Arts Officer:
Ciaran Carson

Scottish Arts Council
12 Manor Place
Edinburgh
EH3 7DD
Tel: 0131–226–6051
Literature Director: Walter Cairns

Arts Council of Wales
9 Museum Place
Cardiff
CF1 3NX
Tel: 01222–394711
Literature Director: Tony Bianci

Regional Arts Boards

Your first point of contact for information about poetry in your region and possible support for poetry events is your Regional Arts Board. A list of these with contact people follows:

East Midlands Arts Board
Mountfields House
Epinal Way
Loughborough
Leicestershire
LE11 0QE
Tel: 01509–218292
Literature Officer: Debbie Hicks

Eastern Arts Board
Cherry Hinton Hall
Cherry Hinton Road
Cambridge
CB1 4DW
Tel: 01223–215355
Literature Officer: Don Watson

London Arts Board
Elme House
133 Long Acre
Covent Garden
London
WC2E 9AF
Tel: 0171–240–1313
Literature Officer: John Hampson

North West Arts Board
12 Harter Street
Manchester
M1 6HY
Tel: 0161–228–3062
Literature Officers: Christine
Bridgewood/Marc Collett

Northern Arts Board
9–10 Osborne Terrace
Jesmond
Newcastle-upon-Tyne
NE2 1NZ
Tel: 0191–281–6334
Head of Published and Broadcast Arts:

John Bradshaw

South East Arts Board
10 Mount Ephraim
Tunbridge Wells
Kent
TN4 8AS
Tel: 01892–525210
Literature Officer: Celia Hunt (ext. 210)

South West Arts Board
Bradninch Place
Gandy Street
Exeter
EX4 3LS
Tel: 01392–218188
Director of Media & Published Arts:
David Drake

Southern Arts Board
13 St Clement Street
Winchester
SO23 9DQ
Tel: 01962–855099
Literature Officer: Keiren Phelan

West Midlands Arts Board
82 Granville Street
Birmingham
B1 2LH
Tel: 0121–631–3121
Literature Officer: David Hart

Yorkshire & Humberside Arts Board
21 Bond Street
Dewsbury
WF13 1AX
Tel: 01924–455555
Literature Officer: Steve Deardey

Poetry Libraries and Specialist Organisations

The following organisations have specialist resources, expertise and useful information on poetry:

Book Trust
Book House
45 East Hill
London
SW18 2QZ
Tel: 0181–870–9055
Executive Director: Brian Perman
Information Officer: Huw Mulseed

British Council Literature Department
10 Spring Gardens
London
SW1A 2BN
Tel: 0171–389–4069
Information Officer: Bridgett Laws

Commonwealth Institute
Kensington High Street
London
W8 6NQ
Tel: 0171–603–4535
Head of Commonwealth Resource
Centre: Karen Peters

Northern Poetry Library
Morpeth Library
Gas House Lane
Morpeth
Northumberland
NE61 1TA
Tel: 01670–511165/512385
Literature and Broadcasts Arts Officer:
Nicholas Baumfield

The Poetry Business
The Studio
Byram Arcade
Westgate
Huddersfield
HD1 1ND
Tel: 01484–834840
Directors: Jane Fisher and Peter Sansom

The Poetry Library
Level 5, Royal Festival Hall
South Bank Centre
London
SE1 8XX
Tel: 0171–921–0664
Assistant Librarian: Jackie Leedham

Scottish Poetry Library
Tweeddale Court
14 High Street
Edinburgh
EH1 1TE
Tel: 0131–557–2876
Director: Tessa Ransford

Society of Authors
84 Drayton Gardens
London
SW10 9SB
Tel: 0171–373–6642

The Poetry Society

The Poetry Society is a national membership body open to all which exists to help poets and poetry thrive in Britain today. It publishes Poetry Review and Poetry News quarterly, has an information and imagination service and runs promotions and educational projects.

Information Service

The Information Service aims to help as many people as possible with their queries about poetry. Information is gathered and regularly updated; computerised records are kept on a database. Users of the service include poets, promoters of poetry, regional and national media, members of the society, those who want to be published and readers of poetry. The aim is to be able to answer all queries efficiently or to be able to pass the query on to an appropriate organisation.

Poetry News

This quarterly newsletter has information, tips, useful contacts and listings of events. There is a 'letters page' and members are actively encouraged to comment on poetry and the Poetry Society. *Poetry News* represents the grassroots end of Poetry Society activity. *Poetry News* is distributed to members and friends of the Poetry Society as well as to key people involved in the arts and literature. It is also included in the Information Pack.

Poets' Register

Got a question about a poet? The Poets' Register is a database containing information on over 1,500 published and performance poets working in the UK or who have a strong connection with the UK poetry scene. Information is kept on reading fees, publication history, willingness and experience to conduct workshops and residencies as well as biographical information and contact addresses.

Open House

The Information Service has recently moved down to the ground floor of the building in Covent Garden as part of the Poetry Society's new open door policy. The ground floor room is an exhibition and browsing space featuring work from poetry groups around the country and beyond. The room can also be used for book launches and receptions as well as open evenings for members. There is a small sales outlet for back issues of *Poetry Review* and other Poetry Society publications (competition anthologies, BP Teachers' Resources Files, etc.).

Information Pack

This information pack is constantly being reviewed and updated. The service also holds information on a range of other subjects from competitions and venues through to who's who at the Arts Councils and how to publish verse in greetings cards. The Society is expanding their *How To . . .* series to include *How To Set Up and Run a Poetry Group* and are continually adding to the Information Sheets series.

Membership

Poetry Society membership is run by the Information Officer to ensure that the Society is as responsive to members' needs as possible. The Society is also committed to reaching out to as many people and groups of people as possible through its various membership schemes and series of workshops and seminars open to members.

Education membership (individuals £24, schools £30) includes a quarterly bulletin on ideas for poetry in the classroom plus *Poetry Review* plus *Poetry News*.

Library membership (£40) includes *Poetry Review*, *Poetry News* and the 'Poetry Friendly Library' resources pack with regular updates.

Education Department

Poetry Society Education aims to bring poetry alive in the classroom and to ensure that poetry is accessible to all young people whether in a formal educational setting or not! By joining the Poetry Society as an education member you will be kept up to date with current education trends, with what's happening in poetry as well as workshop ideas and helpful advice and information. Detailed below are the projects and resources available from Poetry Society Education.

Education membership

Teacher members receive:

- *Poetry Review*;
- *Poetry News*;
- Discounts on selected poetry events and festivals;
- An informative and lively teachers' newsletter and young writers' page;
- Discounts on teachers' workshops;
- Discounts on the publications of Poetry Society Education;
- Advance booking information on seminars and courses.

B.P. Teachers' Poetry Resources Files

The Resources Files are a practical guide for the teaching of poetry in the classroom, containing imaginative ideas as well as a comprehensive reference section. Both primary and secondary versions are available. Special sections for schools in Wales, including a Welsh language translation, are available free of charge.

The Resources Files are funded by BP and have been produced by Poetry Society Education with the support and advice of the Department for Education and officers of the HMI and NCC.

How to Order: B.P. Resources Files cost £12.95 (plus £4 p&p). Send a cheque to the Poetry Society, stating whether you would prefer the primary or secondary files, or send us an official order so that we can invoice your school or institution. Update sets cost £5 each (inclusive of p&p).

Resources Files Updates

The Resources Files are not a static teaching aid: updates come out annually and keep teachers informed of the latest approaches to poetry, competitions, events, texts, and writing schemes.

- Update sets concentrate on extended poetry projects and creative writing;
- Reading and responding to poetry, approaches to pre-20th-century poetry, multi-cultural poetry and poetry and the environment;
- Poetry and information technology, and poetry and special needs teaching.

W H Smith Poets and Schools Scheme

Established in 1971, this very popular scheme is designed to stimulate young people to write their own poetry under the guidance of visiting poets. Poets in Schools, open to all primary, secondary and special needs schools, funds three visits by a poet/poets within one term. Visits are arranged by the Poetry Society in consultation with the schools. In addition to funding all professional fees and expenses in the scheme, W H Smith provides £50 for the school to produce an anthology of the best poems written by the young poets or to purchase book tokens for the participating children.

How to apply: send a letter of application in the first three weeks of the term preceding the one in which you wish to take part. Applications are dealt with on a first come, first served basis.

Projects

Poetry Society Education is committed to challenging young people's experiences of poetry and to developing their skills of expression through innovative creative writing projects. Recently the W H Smith Poets in Schools scheme has brought school children into contact with poets and dancers from the Irie! Theatre Company; documented the history of Cornish industry in an outdoor education project in Camborne; and investigated links between poetry and music in collaboration with the Halle Orchestra's Manchester Gamelan and the Wigmore Hall's Britten Festival. The Poetry Society and the Britten Sinfonia undertook a unique project in two Cambridge schools: children worked with the poet Mick Gowar and the composer Simon Bainbridge to reproduce *Façade for the Nineties*, a reworking of William Walton's *Façade*. Similar projects, such as the creation of a new opera by and for children, are frequently underway.

Advice and Information

The Education Department can provide you with information on all aspects of poetry in education, including:

- Regional lists of poets who work in schools plus detailed biographical information on each poet;
- How to organise a Poets in Schools visit plus information on funding these visits;
- Advice and ideas for running a book festival or poetry week;
- Up-to-date recommended reading lists – including teaching resources;
- Referral to other useful organisations;
- Information for young writers;
- Details of current competitions for young people.

The Education Department can provide information on poets who work in specialist areas of education. Currently available are lists of poets with experience of working with: Visual Arts-Music-Drama-Foreign Languages-Special Needs. Also available: poets with experience of In-service Training and Multi-Cultural poets.

Poetry Society Anthologies

Ten Bananas More!, ed. Sally Bacon and Susan Blishen (Simon & Schuster, 1994) £9.99.
This anthology is based on the *Not Just Kids Stuff* tour (organised by the Poetry Society)
and features poets who write for both adults and children.

Chasing the Sun, ed. Sally Bacon (Simon & Schuster, 1992) £8.99.
An original collection which takes the reader on a voyage of poetry around the world.
Includes the work of many poets working on the Poets in Schools scheme.

Crosscurrents, ed. Pel Plowden (Poetry Society Publications, 1994) £3.95.
A collection of poems written by young people from France, the Republic of Ireland and
England during the project Broadening the Frontiers of Poetry. Includes introductions
and poems from the three poets involved – it is a useful classroom resource which can
also be used as an interesting exercise in translation!

Poetry Review

Poetry Review is the UK's most widely read poetry magazine on developments in
contemporary British and international poetry. It is an excellent classroom resource for
secondary schools and the following two editions are of special interest to teachers:

Vol. 84/1, Spring 1994, New Generation Poets – £4.95
Dedicated to 20 of the best new poets. The New Generation promotion attracted
considerable media and critical interest. Some of the poets will be able to take part in the
Poets in Schools scheme.

Vol. 82/4, Winter 1992/3, Not Just Kids' Stuff – £4.50
Includes articles on writing children's poetry, on new poetry books for children, and
poems by Kit Wright and Grace Nichols.

For further information about the activities of Poetry Society Education please contact:
Martin Drewe, Education Assistant, Poetry Society Education,
22 Betterton Street
London WC2H 9BU
Tel: 0171 240 4810 Fax: 0171 240 4818

Poetry Library

ROYAL FESTIVAL HALL, SOUTH BANK CENTRE,
LONDON SE1 8XX. TEL: 0171–928–0943
OPEN: every day (including Sundays) 11 a.m. to 8.00 p.m.

The Poetry Library has been variously described as 'one of London's best kept secrets', as 'one of the pure flowerings of the imagination for which the English are so seldom given credit,' and as 'the Library that never closes'. It is, in fact, a free public library devoted to the collection and preservation of twentieth-century poetry in the English language. It is a national resource, founded by the Arts Council in 1953, and funded publicly since. Though not a depository library, it aims to acquire all contemporary British poetry published since 1912, including all small press material, privately printed books, kitchen-table publications, etc., so that the obscure and minor poets, difficult to find elsewhere, are kept alongside the best known writers. Although aiming to be comprehensive as far as British material is concerned, it is also an international collection, with almost all Irish poetry and a very wide range from America.

The Library always buys two copies of its selections, putting one permanently in the reference collection and making the other available for loan. The fact that it is a public lending library is central to the Library's ethos in supporting and promoting poetry and making it as accessible as possible. And the Poetry Library is one of the most accessible libraries anywhere, situated in the Royal Festival Hall in London's South Bank Centre and open nine hours a day, seven days a week. Membership is free of charge and open to all UK residents irrespective of whether they live in London or not. For those who cannot visit in person, the national Inter-Library Loans network enables them to borrow via their local library.

The Library also takes a leading role in the dissemination of information on all poetry-related matters, and anyone who has regular recourse to modern poetry for work or for pleasure will sooner or later come across the Library's information service. Current awareness lists on all manner of relevant areas are produced, e.g. poetry magazines, competitions, bookshops, groups and workshops, festivals, evening classes, etc.; they are updated regularly and available to all on receipt of an SAE. The Enquiry Service deals with an almost unquantifiable range of questions on poets and poetry, and is used extensively by radio, television, the newspapers, publishers, schools and the general public.

Following the move to the South Bank Centre in 1988, it became possible to introduce all kinds of new facilities, the most significant being the Audio Visual Collection. Poetry on cassette, record and video is collected in the same way as the books, with two copies purchased, one for reference and one for loan. Listening facilities allow the AV collection to be used in the Library and the collection has grown in the past four years to include over 1,000 items.

The Poetry Library is a unique resource for teachers wishing to stimulate pupils to enjoy the reading and writing of poetry. The children's section contains:

- Books, tapes and videos of poetry for children;
- Free booklets of selected poetry books for each age group;
- Information on competitions;
- Teaching poetry. Sections with ideas for the classroom;
- Listings of poetry on individual themes.

To support teachers in making the most of a visit to the Poetry Library (as well as helping them to fulfil the requirements of the National Curriculum in English), the South Bank Centre Education Department has produced a set of eight work packs each on a different theme. Each pack contains:

- 15 different activities, relating to an overall theme, designed for use by pupils across the age and ability range for Key Stages 1, 2 and 3;
- Teachers' notes for preparation and follow-up work in connection with a visit to the Poetry Library and the activities;
- Lists of volumes and anthologies used in the activities;
- A guide for pupils on how to use the different kinds of indexes found in poetry books;
- Information on what is available at the Poetry Library and a description of the shelf arrangement;
- Packs are available under the following themes: Food ♦ Animals ♦ Places ♦ People ♦ Traditions ♦ Light and Dark ♦ Friends and Enemies ♦ Magic and Mystery.

The packs will be sent in advance free of charge to teachers booking a school visit to the Library.

The Poetry Library is constantly seeking new ways to bring people and poetry together and is dedicated to serving the needs of all poetry readers, be they obsessive or occasional. It always helps to have other librarians aware of the service and to know there is somewhere to refer their enquiries for small press material, and to pass on their frustrating 'Lost Quotations'.

Northern Poetry Library

THE WILLOWS, MORPETH, NORTHUMBERLAND, NE61 1TA.
TEL: 01670–512385
OPEN every day except Sundays and Thursdays
Saturdays – mornings only
Group or class visits are welcome

The aim of the Northern Poetry Library is to make it easy to read modern poetry, wherever you live in the north of England

The Northern Poetry Library was created in 1968 and aims to acquire all books of poetry in English by living writers published in the United Kingdom. Anyone who lives in the region currently covered by Cleveland, Cumbria, Durham, Northumberland and Tyne and Wear can be a member. (If you live outside this region you can become an associate member.)

Membership is free and you can borrow books by post as well as by visiting the Library, which is housed in Morpeth Library, Northumberland. The Library also provides magazines, information on poets and poetry, and access to *English Poetry*, the database. The Northern Poetry Library is the most comprehensive collection of contemporary poetry in England outside London – a resource full of the pleasure of words and creativity.

The Library currently contains around 13,000 books and magazines with more added every month. There are books by individual poets, from the unknown to the famous: everything published since 1968 and many books published before 1968. Special efforts are made to obtain books written by the region's poets.

Then there are anthologies of poetry: selections which can be a very enjoyable way of finding out who and what you might like. Love, death, politics . . . green poetry, new poetry, poetry from Hull and poetry from Wales, sonnets, limericks, long poems, concrete poems . . . any kind of poem can be found through the anthology collection.

Poetry in translation is collected, so the works of many writers around the world are available. Poetry for children and young people is also acquired: books which are often exciting to look at as well as to read.

The Northern Poetry Library takes a wide range of magazines, from the well established to newly published. The Library aims to acquire every magazine in the region and all can be borrowed. Poetry magazines give writers a chance to get published – so if you are a writer, using the Library can help you find out which is the best magazine to send your poems to – and they give readers a chance to discover the latest writing. They also provide interesting information about poets and the poetry world. Many are illustrated with startling original art work.

A special resource of the Library is a database called *English Poetry*. It contains the full texts of all English poetry from 600 to 1900, as listed in the *Cambridge Bibliography of English Literature*. The complete works of Chaucer, Shelley, Tennyson ... a phenomenal 1,350 poets in all.

The database, on CD ROM, can be searched by keyword, author and date (amongst other terms) and the full texts of the poems can be printed out. A whole new world of creative links can be discovered through this facility, and all members of the Northern Poetry Library have access to it. There is usually someone available in the Library to show members how to use the computer.

Scottish Poetry Library

TWEEDDALE COURT, 14 HIGH STREET,
EDINBURGH, EH1 1TE. TEL: 0131–557–2876
OPEN: Mondays, Tuesdays, Wednesdays 12 noon to 6.00 p.m.
Thursdays 2 p.m. to 8.00 p.m.
Saturdays 11 a.m. to 5.00 p.m.

The Scottish Poetry Library is the place for poetry in Scotland. For the regular reader, the serious student or the casual browser, the Library has much to offer.

Since its foundation in 1984 the Scottish Poetry Library has amassed a remarkable collection of written works as well as tapes and videos.

The emphasis is on 20th-century poetry written in Scotland; in Scots, Gaelic and English. Older Scottish poetry is also to be found and contemporary works from almost every part of the world. All of these resources are readily accessible plus advice and information.

The Library provides a service throughout Scotland and not just for those who can visit the premises in Edinburgh. Through its branches, mailing system for borrowing and a travelling collection by van, the material of the Library is within reach of everyone.

Poetry's international importance is recognised and promoted by the Library. Attention is particularly given to minority cultures with similarities to Scotland. Most of the world is represented with texts in English translation or in bilingual editions.

Everyone is welcome at the Library. You can browse leisurely through the shelves or look at the regular exhibitions on varying poetic themes. The notice board is crammed with information about readings, writing groups and workshops, poetry competitions and other news.

Borrowing at the Library is free but there is a charge of 50 pence per item for postal loans – which includes a return label. The catalogue of the lending collection can be purchased for £5.00.

Expert advice is available and specialist lists and bibliographies can be produced with the aid of the Library's special computer program, INSPIRE.

There is a Reading Room above the Library for members. It has a unique collection of literary magazines for reference, and audio-visual equipment donated by British Telecom. This room can be used by visiting groups by prior arrangement. Groups are encouraged to visit Tweeddale Court and the Library can also pay visits in its van. Enquiries are invited from any organisation.

The mainstay of the Scottish Poetry Library Association is its membership. Members are welcome to participate actively in the work of the Association and are kept informed by a regular newsletter.

Getting Poetry Published

It is important to value children's poetry and to publish it attractively within school or the local community. Local libraries are often willing to mount displays of attractively produced work. Schemes such as the WH Smith sponsored Poets in Schools offer some financial support for the production of anthologies, but only a small amount of finance is needed to produce a professional-looking, desktop-published booklet.

The Writers and Artists Yearbook (available for reference in most libraries) gives a listing of those publishers who produce books of poetry and of poetry magazines. There are, however, some magazines which publish children's work exclusively. The following are always ready to consider high quality poetry by young writers:

O WRITE
Frankley Community High School
Pathways Publications,
New Street, Rubery, Rednal, Birmingham B45 0LD.

POPOCATEPETL
100 Cherry Garden Street,
Rotherhithe, London SE16 4PB.

TANDEM
13 Stephenson Road,
Barbourne, Worcester WR1 3EB.

Poetry Competitions for Children

Poetry competitions can provide an important focus for activity and motivation and (for the successful) the satisfactions of publication. Throughout the year there are various, national, regional and local competitions that take place, though these change frequently. The local library, Regional Arts Association, The Poetry Society and the Poetry Library are all important sources for up-to-date information. The Poetry Library publishes a list of the main poetry competitions for children. The following important competitions should be considered.

WH Smith Young Writers' Competition

Anyone in Britain who is not yet 17 years old may enter the WH Smith Young Writers' Competition, with poems, stories, articles or plays.

Between 90 and 100 prizes will be awarded: 30 go to schools for sending in entries of a high overall standard and the rest to individual young writers. In the spring the individual winners will have their work published by Macmillan in a paperback book. As well as the prizes, several hundred certificates of commendation will be awarded.

Stories or poems can be about anything children choose but should not be longer than 3,500 words.

Entries should be children's own work. The panels of judges are looking for signs of real originality in what children write about, and how they write. They are looking for freshness of vision and expression and for honesty. Children are encouraged to write about their own experiences, their own feelings, own imaginings, and find a way of expressing them which is theirs and nobody else's.

While details of the competition may vary from year to year the following timetable is unchanging:

1. It is launched in the first week of October, at which time every school in the country is sent a leaflet by the mailing company, Education Direct. In addition, those schools which ask to be on the WH Smith 'personal' mailing list are mailed independently – the advantage to this is that they can target individual teachers (and keep a track of them when they change school!) and send sufficient leaflets for each member of staff in the school or the English Department.
2. The deadline is always the last Saturday in February of the following year.
3. The final judging takes place in the first week of June – as early as possible.
4. Winners and runners-up are notified in the second week of June.
5. Results are announced at the end of the first or second week of July.

BBC Radio 4 Young Poetry Competition
(in association with The Poetry Society)

BBC Radio 4 looks for the next generation of Radio Poets through its Young Poetry Competition.

The BBC Radio 4 Young Poetry Competition offers four age categories:

19–24 years
16–18 years
12–15 years
8–11 years

The winners of each age group will have their poems broadcast on Radio 4's 'Poetry Please!' as well as receiving a £200 cash prize.

The competition is launched in June and closes in October. For further information please send an SAE to, BBC Radio 4, Young Poetry Competition, BBC, Whiteladies Road, Bristol BS8 2LR.

The Roald Dahl Foundation Poetry Competition

The Roald Dahl Foundation Poetry Competition is run in conjunction with School Books Fairs Ltd and publishers Random House Children's Books.

The aim of the poetry competition is to encourage and stimulate poetry writing in young people under the age of 18 and, besides generous cash and book prizes, offers the opportunity to be published in a book containing the winning entries.

In the first year of the competition, over 10,000 children submitted their poems and almost 200 budding poets saw their poetry in print when the winning entries were published by Red Fox Children's Books in a collection called Wondercrump Poetry.

Who can enter?

Anyone under 18 is eligible for the competition, which is divided into four age groups: 7 years and under; 8–11 years; 12–14 years; 15–17 years. Entries can be submitted privately or through schools, but are limited to one per person. The competition closes in October each year. For full details and entry form contact: The Roald Dahl Foundation Poetry Competition, Random House Children's Books, PO Box 4313, London SW1V 2SG.

Index of Titles

99 Poems in Translation – An
    Anthology 98
All Change 20
All in the Family 80
All-Nite Café, The 17
An Early Start to Poetry 124
Animal Poems 100
Another Custard Pie 27
Another Fifth Poetry Book 73
Another First Poetry Book 70
Another Fourth Poetry Book 72
Another Second Poetry Book 71
Another Third Poetry Book 72
Another Very First Poetry Book 70
Apple Fire 98
Armful of Bears, An 54

B.P. Poetry Resources File for Primary
    Schools 127
B.P. Teachers' Poetry Resources File for
    Secondary Schools 126
Back by Midnight 32
Bananas in Pyjamas 63
Barley, Barley 48
Bears Don't Like Bananas 43
Bed Book, The 40
Beowulf 8
Best of Children's Poetry, The 66
Big bulgy fat black slugs 2
Birds, Beasts and Fishes 61
Blake's Songs of Innocence and
    Experience 124
Blue Poetry Paintbox, A 78
Boo to a Goose 32
Bright Ideas: Inspirations for Poetry 115
Bright Star Shining – Poems for
    Christmas 86
Brontosaurus Chorus, A 54

Brown Parrots of Providencia, The 2
Buy a penny ginger and other rhymes 82
By the Pricking of My Thumbs 64

Calling of Kindred, The 110
Calypso Alphabet, The 1
Cambridge Contemporary Poets 1 119
Cambridge Contemporary Poets 2 119
Cambridge Poetry Box: Teacher's Book
    111
Cambridge Poetry Workshop 14+ 125
Cambridge Poetry Workshop GCSE 125
Cambridge Poetry Workshop Keystage
    3 125
Can it be True? 20
Can't Get to Sleep – Poems to Read at
    Bedtime 6
Candy and Jazzz 48
Caribbean Dozen, A 52
Castle Poems 77
Cat Poems 91
Catapults and Kingfishers 112
Chasing the Sun 53
Cheating at Conkers 95
Child's Garden of Verses, A 45
Cohen's Cornucopia 61
Collected Poems (of W.H. Auden) 4,
    (of Norman McCaig) 26, (of Louis
    MacNeice) 28
Collected Poems: 1909–1962 (T.S.
    Eliot) 12
Collected Poems: Dylan Thomas 113
Collins Book of Nursery Rhymes, The
    90
Come on into my Tropical Garden 34
Come on, Wind 31
Come Rock with I 65
Complete Poems 33
Crazy Cousins 29

Croco'Nile 14
Cup of Starshine, A 56

D.H. Lawrence, Selected Poems 118
Dancing Teepees 103
Dare You Go? 9
Dinner with the Spratts 19
Dinosaur Poems 73, 74
Dog Poems 91
Dog's Dinner 42
Doin Mi Ed in: Rap Poems 96
Don't Do That! 63
Don't Step on that Earwig 103
Dove on the Roof 68
Down at the Dinosaur Fair 3
Dragon Poems 73, 74
Dragonsfire 34
Dream Time 62
Duppy Jamboree 5

Earthways – Poems on Conservation 93
Egg Poems 74
Emergency Poems 74
Every Man Will Shout 52
Everyone loves the Moon 49

Faber Book of 20th Century Women's
    Poetry, The 51
Faber Book of Children's Verse, The
    102
Faber Book of Modern Verse, The 100
Favershams, The 16
Feeling Beastly – Funny Verse to Read
    Aloud 6
Feeling Peckish 7
Fifth Poetry Book, A 73
First Poetry Book, A 70
First things 3
Five Modern Poets 111
Flying Spring Onion, The 46
For Laughing Out Loud 99
Forms of Poetry, The 109
Four Metaphysical Poets 125
Four o'clock Friday 13
Fourth Poetry Book, A 72
Fox on the Roundabout, The 39
Fox Poems 76

Gangsters, Ghosts and Dragonflies 97
Gargling with Jelly (tape) 129

Geoffrey Chaucer: General Prologue to
    the Canterbury Tales 118
Gerard Manley Hopkins: Selected
    Poems 117
Giant Poems 76
Giggly Rhymes 97
Golden Apples 106
Golden Treasury of Nursery Rhymes, A
    (tape) 128
Green Poetry Paintbox, A 78

Heroes and Villains 38
Hey World, Here I Am! 25
Highwayman, The 37
Hippopotamus Dancing and other
    poems 34
Home Poems 74

I Din Do Nuttin 1
I Like That Stuff 104
I Never Saw A Purple Cow 61
I Remember, I Remember 9
I Saw Esau 94
In Love: a collection of love poems 67
Ink-Slinger 104
Inky Pinky Ponky 101
Is that the New Moon? 65
It's a Mad, Mad World 64
It's Halloween 41

Jack and Jill: A Book of Nursery
    Rhymes 68
Jigglewords 3
Jingle Jangle 105
Jocasta Carr, Movie Star 15
John Donne, Selected Poems 117
Josephine and Pobble 14
Jungle Jingles 24
Junk Mail 17

Kid 3
Knock Down Ginger 33

Lady of Shalott, The 47
Last Rabbit, The 66
Late Again, Mai Ling? 5
Laughter is an Egg (tape) 128
Lavender's Blue 91
Let's Celebrate: Festival Poems 81
Life Doesn't Frighten Me At All 51

Like it or Not   13
Little Miss Muffet   4

Machine Poems   58
Mad Parrot's Countdown, The   33
Magic Tree, The   108
Meet My Folks!   22
Messages   90
Midnight Forest with Magic Mirror   36
Midnight Party, The   5
Mik's Mammoth   15
Milton: Comus and Other Poems   122
Mimi and Apricot Max   14
Mind the Gap   43
Minibeast Poems   74
Minibeasts, A Book of Poems   68
Mink War, The   23
Missing Bear   30
Monkey Poems   75
Moon Frog   10
Moon-Whales   21
More Giggly Rhymes   97
Morning Break   30
Mother Gave a Shout   103
Mother Goose   69
Mother Goose – A Collection of Nursery
    Rhymes   106
Mouse Poems   76
My Brother's A Beast   64
My Granny is a Sumo Wrestler   39

Narrative Poems   84
Never Say Boo to a Ghost and other
    haunting rhymes   81
New Angles, Book 1   79
New Angles, Book 2   80
New Dragon Book of Verse, The   85
New Kid on the Block, The   41
New Poetry, The   89
New Selected Poems, 1966–1987   87
New Where's That Poem?, The   121
Night Photograph   16
Nightmares Poems to Trouble your
    Sleep   41
Nineteenth and Twentieth Century
    Verse   126
Noah's Ark   27
Noisy Poems   58
Nursery Collection, The   21
Nursery Rhymes – Book One   90

Nursery Rhymes – Book Two   90

Oh, How Silly!   62
Oh, That's Ridiculous!   62
Old Possum's Book of Practical Cats   12
One of Your Legs is Both The Same   92
One, Two, Buckle My Shoe and Other
    Favourite Rhymes (tape)   129
Oranges and Lemons   89
Oscar the dog and friends   8
Our Favourite Rhymes   92
Out and About   21
Out of the Blue   37, 106
Over in the Meadow   47
Owl and the Pussy Cat, The   24
Owls and Pussy-Cats   25
Oxford Book of Animal Poems, The   83
Oxford Book of Children's Verse, The
    95
Oxford Book of Christmas Poems, The
    83
Oxford Book of Poetry for Children   59
Oxford Book of Story Poems, The   84
Oxford Nursery Rhyme Book, The   94
Oxford Student Texts   117
Oxford Treasury of Children's Poems,
    The   85

Packet of Poems, A   56
Peace and War   87
Peacock Pie   30
Pedalling Man, The   20
People Poems   57
Pet Poems   69
Phantom Lollipop Lady, The   19
Pillow Talk (tape)   128
Pizza, Curry, Fish and Chips   44
Play Rhymes   60
Poems 1   86
Poems 2   86, 120
Poems for Christmas   58
Poems from other Centuries   123
Poems from the Sac Magique   38
Poems in Focus   120
Poems in my Earphone   52
Poems of Wilfred Owen, The   123
Poems that Go Bump in the Night   92
Poems That Point the Finger   13
Poetry   119
Poetry Corner 2   55

Poetry of Protest, The   82
Poetry of War, The   82
Poetry Readings   113
Poetry Street 1, 2 and 3   96
Poets of the Century   105
Pope: The Rape of the Lock   117
Pot of Gold, A   57
Pudding and Pie   107
Pussy Cat, Pussy Cat   63

Quartet of Poems   116

Racing the Wind   2
Ragged Robin   42
Rainbow   47
Rattle Bag, The   88
Read a Poem, Write a Poem   118
Red Poetry Paintbox, A   78
Rhinestone Rhino   19
Rhythm of Our Days   114
Ride a Cock Horse   107
Rosie and the Rustlers   15
Round and Round the Garden   107

Said the Mouse to the Elephant   98
Say Hello to the Buffalo   16
Say it Again Granny   1
School Poems   74
School's Out   78
Scrumdiddly   66
Sea Poems   75
Season Songs   22
Second Poetry Book, A   71
Secrets: A collection of poems from
    hidden worlds   10
Seed Poems   74
Selected Poems   4
Selected Poems 1957–1981 (Ted
    Hughes)   22
Serious Concerns   7
Sing a Song of Sixpence – popular
    nursery rhymes   65
Singing Down The Breadfruit   46
Snail Song   36
Something Big Has Been Here   40
Song of the City   39
Space Poems   75
Spaceways   80
Speaking for Ourselves   37
Spenser, The Faerie Queene, Book 1   110

Splinters   83
Sports Poems   74
Squeeze Words Hard   109
Stack of Story Poems, A   60
Star Poems   77
Steel Drums and other Stories and Poems
    from around the World   25
Steps to Poetry   114
Storm's Eye   36
Story of Daniel, The   26
Strawberry Drums   93
Surprise, Surprise   29
Sylvia Plath: Collected Poems   40

Take Me Like I Am   63
Tasty Poems   59
Ten Bananas More!   53
Tennyson: Selected Poems   121
Them and Us – Pairs of poems for young
    and old   67
There's a Poet Behind You   112
There's an Awful Lot of Weirdos in our
    Neighbourhood   28
Thin Ice   117
Third Poetry Book, A   71
Thirteen Secrets of Poetry, The   31
This is the Bear   18
This is the Bear and the Picnic Lunch   18
This is the Bear and the Scary Night   18
Thomas Hardy: Selected Poems   118
Three Books: Remains of Elmet; Cave
    Birds; River   23
Through A Window   59
Tiny Tim   57
Toffee Pockets: Poems for Children   49
Touched With Fire   116
Trade Winds   88
Transport Poems   75
Twiddling Your Thumbs   7
Twinkle Twinkle Chocolate Box   79
Twins Poems   77

Verse Universe   55
Verse Universe 2   55
Very First Poetry Book, A   69

W.B. Yeats: Selected Poems   117
Wake Up   31
Walk the High Wire   102

Walker Book of Poetry for Children, The 99

Walker Book of Read-Aloud Rhymes for the Very Young, The 99

Walking on Air 10

Walkmen have Landed, The 45

Water Poems 78

Water, Water 32

Way to the Zoo, The 89

We're Going on a Bear Hunt 44

Welcome To The Party 101

West Indian Poetry 122

What is a Kumquat? 8

What On Earth . . .? 93

When Did You Last Wash your Feet? 43

Where's My Teddy? 2

Whisked Away 6

Whispers from a Wardrobe 11

Whitsun Weddings, The 24

Who Do You Think You Are? 108

Who's Been Sleeping in My Porridge? 28

Wiggle Waggle 35

William Wordsworth: Selected Poems 117

Wish You Were Here? 35

Witch's Brew, The 29

Wizard Poems 74

Word Party, The 11

WordPlay 54

WordPlay 2 54

Words for All Seasons 101

Words on a Faded T-shirt 45

Words with Wrinkled Knees 12

Wordspells 94

Wordsworth – Prelude I, II etc 112

Wordsworth and Coleridge: Lyrical Ballads 121

Writing Poems 115, 123

Year Full of Poems, A 84

Yellow Poetry Paintbox, A 78

You'll Love This Stuff! 104

Young Dragon Book of Verse 85

Yuck! 3

Index of Authors and Editors

Abbs, Peter 109
Adcock, Fleur 51
Agard, John 1, 51, 52, 128
Alborough, Jez 2
Alcorn, Maureen 109
Allen, Fergus 2
Andrew, Moira 2
Anstey, Sarah 117
Armitage, Simon 3
Armstrong, Isobel 52
Astbury, Anthony 98
Auden, W.H. 4

Bacon, Sally 53
Baker, Catherine 54
Barlow, Adrian 110
Bayley, P.C. 110
BBC Publications 54, 55
Beck, Ian 4, 107
Bennett, Jill 56, 57, 58, 59
Bleiman, Barbara 111
Blishen, Edward 59
Blishen, Susan 53
Bloom, Valerie 5
Body, Wendy 5, 59
Bradman, Tony 60
Brown, Marc 60, 99
Brown, Richard 5, 6
Burgess, Mark 6, 7

Carroll, Lewis 25
Carter, Ann 61
Chichester Clark, Emma 61
Cohen, Mark 61
Cole, William 62
Cook, Helen 62, 63, 64, 65, 104, 111, 112
Cope, Wendy 7, 65

Corbett, Pie 112
Cotton, John 2, 8
Cowling, Sue 8
Cross, Vince 65
Crossley-Holland, Kevin 8
Cullimore, Stan 5
Cunliffe, John 9
Curry, Jennifer 9, 66, 67, 68

Darbishire, Helen 112
Davey, Gwenda Beed 68
Davies, Walford 113
Doherty, Berlie 2, 10
Dunmore, Helen 10

Ebborn, Amanda 109
Edwards, Richard 10, 11
Eliot, T.S. 12
Esbensen, Barbara Juster 12
Ewart, Gavin 13

Farrow, Rob 9
Feeney, Peter 117
Fisher, Robert 68, 69
Forbes, Duncan 13
Foreman, Michael 69
Foster, John 13, 69, 70, 71, 72, 73, 74, 75, 76, 77, 78, 79, 80, 81
Fry, Don 113
Fuller, Simon 82

Geras, Adèle 14
Gerrard, Roy 14, 15, 16
Gibson, Miles 16
Gill, Richard 117
Glynn, Martin 96
Godbert, Geoffrey 98
Gray, Cecil 122
Green, Veronica 114

Greenlaw, Lavinia   16
Griffin, John   114
Grimshaw, Nigel   114
Gross, Philip   17
Groves, Paul   114
Gurr, Elizabeth   117

Hadley, Helen   115
Hallworth, Grace   82
Harrison, Michael   17, 83, 84, 85, 86,
   87, 115
Hayes, Sarah   18
Healy, Maura   116
Heaney, Seamus   87, 88
Heath, R.B.   88
Henri, Adrian   19
Hill, Susan   20
Hoban, Russell   20
Houston, Libby   20
Hughes, Shirley   21
Hughes, Ted   21, 22, 23, 88
Hulse, Michael   89
Hydes, Jack   116

Jackson, David   89
Jordan, Paul   120

Kemp, Gene   23
Kennedy, David   89
King, Karen   89
King-Smith, Dick   24
Kitchen, David   117

Langley, Jonathan   90
Larkin, Philip   24
Lear, Edward   24, 25
Lee, Victor   117
Lewis, Naomi   90
Linden, Ann Marie   25
Lines, Kathleen   91
Little, Jean   25
Livingston, Myra Cohn   91

Macbeth, George   26
MacCaig, Norman   26
Mack, Peter   118
MacNeice, Louis   28
Magee, Wes   29, 30, 118, 119
Mansfield, Rogers   52
Mare, Walter de la   30

Markus, Julia   120
Martin, Christopher   120
McClure, Gillian   92
McGough, Roger   27, 128
McKee, David   92
McMullen, Eunice   92
McNaughton, Colin   28
Mendelson, Edward   4
Millgate, Michael   121
Mitchell, Adrian   31, 93
Mole, John   31, 32, 33
Moore, Marianne   33
Morley, David   89
Morris, Helen   121
Moses, Brian   33, 34, 112

Nicholls, Judith   2, 34, 35, 36, 93, 94
Nichols, Grace   34, 52
Noyes, Alfred   37

Opie, Iona   94, 95
Opie, Peter   94, 95
Oram, Hiawyn   37
Orme, David   38, 95, 96
Ousbey, Jack   38
Owen, Gareth   39
Owen, W.J.B.   121

Park, Julie   97
Patten, Brian   97, 129
Patterson, Geoffrey   98
Paul, Korky   73, 81
Pinter, Harold   98
Pirrie, Jill   98
Plath, Sylvia   40
Poetry Society, The   126
Porter, Peter   100
Prelutsky, Jack   40, 41, 99
Prince, F.T.   122

Ramchand, Kenneth   122
Rawnsley, Irene   42
Reeves, James   42
Rice, John   2, 43
Richards, Roy   124
Richardson, John   109
Richardson, Polly   100
Roberts, Michael   100
Roberts, Susan   101
Rogers, Paul   2

Rosen, Michael 43, 44, 101
Rutherford, Meg 100
Rylands, Ljiljana 27

Sale, James 96
Sansom, Peter 123
Saville, Malcolm 101
Sedgwick, Fred 44
Silver, Norman 45
Smith, Janet Adam 102
Sneve, Virginia 103
Sommerville, Rowena 103
Stallworthy, Jon 123
Steele, Susanna 101, 103
Stevenson, Robert Louis 45
Stewart, Pauline 46
Stuart-Clark, Christopher 83, 84, 85, 86, 87, 115
Styles, Morag 62, 63, 64, 65, 103, 104, 111, 112
Sweeney, Matthew 46

Tennyson, Alfred 47
Tissier, Adrian 123
Todd, Jan 118
Torbe, Mike 113

Voce, Louise 47

W.H. Smith Young Writers' Judges 102
Wade, Barrie 47, 48, 105
Walter, Colin 124
Ward, Dave 48
Waters, Fiona 106
Wildsmith, Brian 106
Williams, Sarah 107
Willis, Jeanne 49
Willmott, Richard 118, 124, 125
Wood, Jeffrey 125
Wood, Lynn 125
Woodhead, Chris 126
Woolger, David 108

Young, James 49

Thematic Index

Action rhymes   107
Adolescence   26, 45, 48, 52, 119
Adventure   15, 84
Age   73, 105, 115, 117
Age and death   124
Aliens   28
Alphabets   43, 118
Anger   13
Animal conservation   61
Animal rights   64, 92
Animals   6, 8, 9, 10, 12, 15, 16, 19, 20,
   23, 24, 25, 27, 33, 34, 41, 42, 43, 47,
   52, 55, 59, 61, 66, 69, 70, 71, 72, 73,
   76, 83, 84, 85, 89, 92, 99, 100, 117
April Fool jokes   29
Arcane ritual   23

Babies   104
Ballads   95
Battles   24
Bears   2, 18, 44, 54
Beds   40
Bedtime   7, 21
Beowulf   9
Bible stories   26, 37
Birds   23, 84, 101
Birth   101
Birth and Death   23
Black women poets   116
Body, The   51
Bouncing rhymes   107
Britain in decline   89

Caribbean   1, 25, 34, 46, 52
Caribbean childhood experiences   5
Castles   77
Caterpillar   35
Cats   12, 14, 44, 64, 91

Cave men   15
Celebration   23, 81, 101
Childhood   8, 13, 20, 28, 39, 46, 48,
   52, 63, 68, 70, 71, 86, 87, 88, 91, 119
Children   10, 34, 44, 54, 99, 120
Children and Parents   63
Children's play   29
Christmas   20, 58, 83, 87
Circus   27, 48, 72
Cities   99, 101
Classroom   85
Clothes   52
Colours   38, 101
Comic Verse   28, 39
Common experiences and concerns   24
Computers   52
Conservation   66, 93
Contrasts   117
Counting   5, 47, 118
Counting rhymes   57
Countryside   88
Cowboys   16
Creatures   86, 108
Critical commentaries   122
Crocodiles   15
Crowds   97

Dancing   65, 90
Dancing rhymes   107
Day Out   35
Days and Weeks   118
Death   9, 13, 24, 43, 84, 98, 101
Decay   24
Dinosaurs   28, 54, 73, 74
Dogs   8, 92
Domestic life   104
Dragons   74
Dreams   28, 44, 56, 62, 85, 91, 95
Drivers   38

Drums 97

Early childhood 37
Early concepts 21
Eggs 74
Elements, The 70
Emergencies 74
Environmental issues 13, 17, 19, 52, 60, 73, 115, 124
Exile 98

Fairy Tales 19
Family 13, 22, 37, 39, 40, 41, 43, 55, 60, 64, 70, 71, 72, 73, 81, 91, 104
Family breakdown 13
Famine 88
Fantasy 29, 31, 41, 85
Fear 13, 19, 24
Feelings 10, 115
Festivals 35, 81
Fire 21
Food 7, 20, 21, 55, 59, 67, 99
Football 55
Fox 76
Freedom 88
Friends 54, 55
Fun 97
Furniture 52

Games 32, 90
Gender 82
Getting up 5
Ghosts 9, 19, 33, 39, 42, 81, 84, 92, 108
Ghosts and witches 65
Giants 28, 77
Grandparents 49
Grants 55
Greek/Indian Legend 21
Growing-Up 30, 44, 55
Growth 35

Hallowe'en 41
Hand rhymes 7
Heroes/Heroines 101
Heroism 124
Holidays 55
Home 46, 74, 95, 99
Human behaviour 2, 17, 24
Humour 29, 39, 62, 64, 92, 100, 128

Imprisonment 82
Index of children's poems 121
Individuality 63
Insects 3, 5, 16, 69, 84, 103
Ireland 87

Jewels 57
Journeys 55, 85, 108

Knee-jogging rhymes 107

Land 120
Landscape 27, 73, 86
Language 72, 117
Laughter 128
Letters 55
Life 9
Life cycle 35
Likes and dislikes 13
Limericks 57
Lists 118
Living in today's world 3
London 25
Lost toys 30
Love 8, 13, 20, 27, 37, 51, 67, 88, 98, 117, 120, 124
Lullabies 95, 104, 107

Machines 55, 56, 59
Madness 97
Magic 9, 28, 56, 74, 99, 108, 128
Mammoths 15
Marriage 120
Memories 10
Men 8
Metaphysical poets 125
Mice 76
Minibeasts 69, 74
Modern times 45
Monsters 85
Months 84
Moon 22, 49
Multi-cultural verse 105
Music 108
Myself 55
Mystery 9, 84, 85, 86
Myths and symbols 124

Natural environment 23
Natural world 64, 72, 120

Nature 21, 22, 46, 66, 70, 71, 72, 73, 83, 87, 88, 98, 99, 104, 105, 124
Night 17, 72
Nightmares 42
Noah 28
Noise 58
Nonsense 13, 21, 25, 62, 64, 85, 92
North American Indians 103
Nostalgia 28
Nursery rhymes 66, 69, 90, 91, 92, 106, 107, 128, 129

Opposites 36
Other worlds 55

Parents 54, 120
Past, The 115
Patting and clapping rhymes 107
Peace 87, 88
People 9, 20, 27, 54, 57, 63, 85, 86, 95, 96, 99, 108, 117, 119, 120
Performance 6
Pets 69
Picnics 18
Pirates 28
Places 9, 20
Play 46, 70, 104
Play rhymes 60, 83
Playground rhymes 57, 105
Poetry 9, 73
Poetry Study Guide 109
Poets 59, 96
Politics 43, 89
Possessions 52
Poverty 60, 88
Prejudice 24, 117
Protest 82
Proverbs/Sayings 2
Puddles and mud 21

Race 43, 52, 82
Racism 51
Rap 96
Reading and writing poetry 112
Reflection 86
Reflections 120
Relationships 8, 43, 91, 105
Religion 81
Rescue 38
Rhymes 79

Riddles 32, 33, 95
Ridiculous, The 62
Rocking rhymes 107
Romance 84
Royal persons 108
Rural life 87

School 9, 13, 19, 30, 33, 37, 43, 44, 46, 48, 51, 54, 55, 60, 70, 71, 72, 74, 79, 92, 95, 101, 104, 115, 120, 128
Science 17, 89
Sea, The 17, 72, 75, 85, 108
Sea-side 35
Seascapes 86
Seasons 22, 70, 71, 72, 73, 83, 84, 99, 101
Secrets 10
Seeds 74
Singing 90
Slavery 88
Social history 23
Society 104
Songs 32, 65, 88, 95
Sounds 58
Space 76, 80
Spells and charms 65, 88
Sport 13, 72, 73, 74
Sports Day 55
Stars 77
Stone-age 15
Stories 91
Strangers 55
Sun and Moon 118
Supernatural 42

Tastes 59, 67
Teaching poetry 111
Teenage 45, 51
Time 124
Times past 24
Tongue-twisters 61
Tots 38
Toys 55
Traditional rhymes 25, 69
Traffic 38
Transport 52, 75
Travel 9, 101
Tricksters 55
Twins 28, 42, 77

Urban Scene, The 89

Vampires 81
Victorian families 16
Violence 23, 105
Visitors 108

Waking Up 31
War 20, 68, 72, 73, 82, 86, 87, 88,
    101, 105, 120, 124
Water 32, 78, 104, 120
Water and sand 21
Weather 9, 23, 85, 101, 106
Wild, The 91
Wildlife 104

Wind 21
Witches 92
Women 65
Women in Society 104
Women poets 51
Wonders 95
Word Play 8
Work 88
Writing 27, 104, 115
WWI 120
WWII 120

Young and old 67
Youth 51, 82